California Songbook

with historical commentary

Compiled and edited by Keith & Rusty McNeil

Companion to the recording
California Songs with historical narration Volumes One and Two

WEM Records
Riverside, California

Contents

Immigrants and
Dust Bowl Refugees

World War Two,
Songs of the Cities

Introduction

Folksinger Huddie "Leadbelly" Ledbetter once defined folk songs as "songs folks sing." Rusty and I learned California's history through "songs California folks sing."

My earliest memories are of my mother singing while doing housework and fixing meals. She seemed to have an endless supply of songs packed away in her memory. As I grew older, I found that mom had learned many of these songs from her father, who had learned many of them from his father.

My grandparents on both sides of the family came to California during the gold rush. Music played an important role in their lives, and I grew up with songs from the gold rush and Civil War eras. I remember our family gatherings in Santa Maria when I was a child, singing around the old pump organ played by my cousin Wiff and dancing the schottische, the versuvianne, and square dances.

I learned cowboy songs from my great-uncles Lewie and Ace. Uncle Ace was a cattle rancher who loved to sing and dance. I can still hear him singing as he worked cattle on his horse Prince, alternating between "When the Roll Is Called Up Yonder" and "Rye Whiskey." Uncle Lewie was a cowboy who worked ranches all over California. He sat straight in the saddle, was a magnificent horse trainer and roper, and a crack shot with a rifle. He played the guitar and sang all of the cowboy songs.

My father played piano, violin, harmonica and bones. He spoke Spanish, which he learned from his German mother and his Spanish-speaking playmates, and fell in love with Mexican songs. He courted my mother with "La Paloma" and other songs in Spanish which he learned from the singing of the ranchers and ranch hands in the Pozo area of San Luis Obispo County.

Rusty and I met at the ski lodge in Badger Pass, Yosemite, where we were both working. The summer after we married, we worked at Tuolomne Meadows in the park's high country, where we met Debbie and Al Parducci, who were camping nearby. Debbie was a collector of folk songs, and we shared songs with her all summer. I had never considered the songs my parents sang as folk songs, they were just songs mom and dad sang, but the idea of collecting folksongs was intriguing.

Debbie had planted the seeds that grew to become our life's work.

We began to seek out songs sung by our fellow Californians, many of whose cultural backgrounds and experiences were quite different from ours. We continued to expand our song collecting from California's many sub-cultures, and developed an appreciation for the scope of our state's rich musical, cultural and historical heritage.

In 1966 I resigned as District Plant Manager of Pacific Telephone, and Rusty and I began our careers as interpreters of history through folksong. In 1973 we converted an old school bus into a motor home and, for the next twenty years, spent four to six months each year traveling with our family up and down California and across the United States, collecting songs, teaching continuing education courses at colleges and universities, and performing community concerts and school programs.

I learned most of the early songs in this book from my family. Rusty and I learned the later songs through our work experiences and travels in California, and from friends, students and research throughout the Golden State.

Keith McNeil, Riverside, California, January, 2001.

All songs, unless otherwise specified and credited, are traditional songs arranged and adapted by Keith & Rusty McNeil.

Forward

In Mexico, in 1524, Spanish explorer Hernán Cortés received reports of an island to the north, rich in pearls and gold, and inhabited only by women. Eleven years later, Cortés landed on what he thought was the fabled island, established a settlement, and claimed it for Spain.

Cortés's "island" turned out to be the peninsula of Baja California. There were few pearls and no Amazons, but California became much more important than Cortés's wildest dreams.

Who could have envisioned the myriad of industries in California's future? These industries included the fur trade, gold mining, cattle and sheep ranches, railroads, farms, fishing, motion pictures, oil, ship building, aircraft manufacture, space and computer technology. And who could have predicted that California would become a haven for adventurers, entrepreneurs and refugees from Asia, Europe, the Dust Bowl, Mexico and Central America?

The songs in this volume reflect some of the highlights of California's turbulent history.

"You Who Don't Believe It" was first published in *Put's Golden Songster* in 1858. The author, John A. Stone, called himself "Old Put." He was the most prolific of the gold rush songwriters, and published a number of song books during the 1850s. Old Put came to the California goldfields in 1850, struck gold in 1853, and retired to write songs and play his guitar. He organized a singing group called the "Sierra Rangers," and they toured the mining camps performing his songs. He published his first song book, *Put's Original California Songster*, in 1855.

The tune is "The Blue-Tailed Fly," a popular 19th century minstrel song.

You Who Don't Believe It

Words: John A. Stone. Music: Anonymous.

We've got more gold in all the world,
A flag that wins whene'er unfurled,
And smarter men to help us through,
Than England, France or Mexico.

CHORUS
You who don't believe it,
You who don't believe it,
You who don't believe it,
Come yourselves and see!

We've smarter ships than Johnny Bull,
Larger sheep with finer wool;
A prison too! you cannot fail
To throw a *Bull* through by the tail. CHORUS

We raise the largest cabbage heads,
Got more and better feather beds;
Of everything we've got the best,
And *thieves* until you cannot rest. CHORUS

All ruffianism now is o'er,
The country's safer than before;
Our cities keep the rowdies straight,
Or send them through the Golden Gate. CHORUS

We've got the highest mountains here,
Taller trees and faster deer;
And travel more, at higher rates,
Than people in the Eastern States. CHORUS

We've got the smartest river boats,
And, ten to one, old whiskey bloats;
We're blest with very heavy fogs,
And any amount of *poodle dogs*! CHORUS

We've got a few unmarried gals,
Railroads, ditches and canals;
Although we did repudiate,
A joke 'twas only to create. CHORUS

To one and all, both young and old,
You're welcome to the land of gold;
So come along, be not afraid,
We guarantee you *all* well paid! CHORUS

Indian, Spanish and Mexican California

Mohave Gambling Song

California's first settlers arrived more than ten thousand years ago. Before the first Europeans arrived, California's native population was around 250,000. Most of the people were hunters and gatherers, speaking twenty-one different languages and 135 dialects.

They sang songs, danced, and played drums, rattles, scrapers, flutes and whistles. The Maidu people also played a musical bow by placing one end of the bow against the side of the jaw, using the mouth cavity as a sound chamber and plucking the bow string.

Dancing and singing were integral parts of the basic culture of California's Indians. They sang prayers to the Great Spirit and lullabies to their babies, sang of the changing of the seasons, of birth and death, of hunting and fishing, of the surrounding environment and of war. They sang for ceremonial purposes and for recreation. Songs accompanied games for children and for adults.

This song was collected by James Mooney, and published in the 14th Annual Report, Bureau of Ethnology, 1896. It is a gambling song from the Mohave nation.

Quniáika – Mohave

Mohave Gambling Song

Words and Music: Anonymous.

Yo homaho yo-owa na
Haya mahayama kaniyowi
Yo homaho yo-owa na
Haya mahayama kaniyowe

Muiñeira D' A Fonte

Juan Rodriguez Cabrillo and his crew were the first Europeans to see Alta California (Upper California). In 1542, forced to find shelter during a storm, they landed near Point Conception. Cabrillo invited the local Indian leader and a number of her people to board his ship where they all danced to the music of the *gaita de los Castellanos* and the *tamboril* (Spanish bagpipes and tambourine). These were the first European musical instruments ever seen or heard by native Californians.

"Muiñeira D' A Fonte" is a traditional muiñeira dance tune from the Galicia region of Spain.

Muiñeira D' A Fonte

Music: Anonymous.

Kyrie Eleison

In the late 18th and early 19th centuries, Father Junipero Serra and his Franciscans established a series of missions that extended from San Diego to San Francisco. They quickly capitalized on the musical abilities of the native Californians. Nearly every mission formed an Indian choir and an Indian band complete with violins, viols, trumpets and drums. The choirs chanted the mass using melodies from lively hornpipes, jigs and reels which they learned from passing sailors. At the Mission Santa Cruz they sometimes chanted the mass to the Marseillaise. The mission priests also taught the Indians to sing Gregorian chants.

"Kyrie Eleison" is a traditional Gregorian chant. The Greek words mean: "Lord have mercy, Christ have mercy." The Kyrie is a part of the Roman Catholic mass.

Kyrie Eleison

Words and Music: Anonymous.

Kyrie eleison
Christe eleison
Kyrie eleison

Cielito Lindo

Before the Europeans arrived, each Southwestern Indian nation developed its own musical traditions. As Spanish and other European music merged with Indian music, different regions produced styles which were quite diverse.

"Cielito Lindo" is still popular in California and Mexico. The first version is *norteño*, a musical style popular in the American Southwest and Northern Mexico. The second version is a *huapango* from the Huasteca Indians in Vera Cruz, on the southeast coast of Mexico.

The words to the *norteño* version mean:

From the dark mountain they appear, a pair of forbidding black eyes. Ay, ay, ay, ay! Sing and don't cry, because hearts sing quickly, my love. That beauty mark near your mouth, give it to no one, because it is mine. If the bird that abandons his first nest finds it taken by another, he deserves it. Cupid shot an arrow into the air, and I was the one injured. If your mother tells you to close the door, jingle the key and leave it open. When you fall in love, look first where you place your eyes, so you won't cry later.

Cielito Lindo (Norteño)

Words and Music: Anonymous.

De la Sier - ra Mo - re-na, Cie - li - to Lin-do, vie - nen ba - jan - do, Un par de o - ji - tos ne-gros, Cie - li - to Lin- do, de co-tra - ban- do. ¡Ay, ay, ay, ay! can - ta y no llo - res, por - que can - tan-do se a - le-gran,Cie - li - to Lin-do,los co - ra - zon - es.

De la Sierra Morena, Cielito Lindo, vienen bajando,
Un par de ojitos negros, Cielito Lindo, de contrabando.

CHORUS
¡Ay, ay, ay, ay! Canta y no llores,
Porque cantando se alegran,
Cielito Lindo, los corazones.

Ese lunar que tienes, Cielito Lindo, junto a la boca,
No se lo des a nadie, Cielito Lindo, que a mi me toca. CHORUS

Pájaro que abandona, Cielito Lindo, su primer nido,
Si lo encuentra ocupado, Cielito Lindo, muy merecido. CHORUS

Una flecha en el aire, Cielito Lindo, lanzo Cupido,
Y como fue jugando, Cielito Lindo, yo fui el herido. CHORUS

Si tú mama te dice, Cielito Lindo, cierra la puerta,
Hasle ruido a la llave, Cielito Lindo, y déjala abierto. CHORUS

Siempre que te enamores, Cielito Lindo, mira primero
Donde pones los ojos, Cielito Lindo, no llores luego.

LAST CHORUS
¡Ay, ay, ay, ay! Mira primero,
Donde pones los ojos, Cielito Lindo,
No llores luego.

The words to the *huapango* version mean:

Every Sunday I come to visit you. When will it be Sunday again, my love, so I can return? Ah, how I wish all week long that it was Sunday. Tree of hope, don't weaken. Don't let your eyes weep as I depart, because if I see tears in your eyes, I will not leave. If you doubt my feelings, open my heart with a knife, my love. Ah, but open it with care that you do not hurt yourself, because you are within me. Some say they feel no pain at parting. Tell whoever told you that to bid farewell to the one he loves, and then see how he feels as his tears are falling. Ay, ay, ay!

Cielito Lindo (Huasteca)

Words and Music: Anonymous.

De domingo a domingo te vengo a ver,
Cuando será domingo Cielito Lindo para volver.
¡Ay, ay, ay, ay, ay! Yo bien quisiera,
Que toda la semana, Cielito Lindo, domingo fuera.
¡Ay, ay, ay!

Árbol de la esperanza, mantente firme,
Que no lloren tús ojos, Cielito Lindo, al despedirme,
¡Ay, ay, ay, ay, ay! Porque si miro,
Lágrimas en tús ojos, Cielito Lindo, no me despido.
¡Ay, ay, ay!

Si alguna duda tienes de mi pasión,
Abre con un cuchillo, Cielito Lindo, mi corazón,
¡Ay, ay, ay, ay, ay! Pero con tiento,
Que tu no te làstimes, Cielito Lindo, que estas dentro.
¡Ay, ay, ay!

Dicen que no se siente la despedida,
Dile al quien te lo cuente, Cielito Lindo, que se despida,
¡Ay, ay, ay, ay, ay! Del ser que adora,
Y veras que lo siente, Cielito Lindo, Y hasta que llora.
¡Ay, ay, ay!

The Spanish Fandango

Mexico gained independence from Spain as a result of the Mexican Revolution of 1810-1821, and California became a province of Mexico in 1822. Under Mexican rule, California guaranteed full equality, both political and racial, to all citizens.

California's cowboys, called *vaqueros*, gained world-wide fame for their expert riding and roping skills. In the 1830s, in the Hawaiian Islands, King Kamehameha III hired California *vaqueros* to teach the islanders to work the herds of cattle that were running wild on the islands.

The *vaqueros* brought their guitars and their tradition of tuning them to open chords. The Hawaiians learned the open tunings, and used them to help create the now famous Hawaiian "slack key" guitar styles.

One of the more popular 19th century California melodies using an open tuning was "The Spanish Fandango."

The Spanish Fandango

Music: Anonymous.

Windy Bill

California's Indian and Mexican *vaqueros* made major contributions to the development of the American cowboy. One of these contributions was the western saddle. The Moors had brought saddles from North Africa to Spain after their conquest of that country in the eighth century. The Spaniards refined the Moorish saddle and carried it to the new world. California *vaqueros* further refined it into what we now know as the western saddle.

California *vaqueros* also developed a roping technique in which the cowboy, after roping a steer, took a couple of turns with his rope <u>around</u> the saddle horn instead of tying it to the saddle horn. Anglo cowboys called the turns "dally welters" or "dallies," from the Spanish *da la vuelta*. The dallys allowed their rawhide ropes to give, or slip around the saddle horn when the steer reached the end. This prevented the rope from breaking, the saddle from being ripped off the horse, or the horse from being thrown off its feet.

In the song "Windy Bill," the Texas cowboy pays a price for neglecting to rope California style. The term "withers" refers to the juncture of the shoulder bones of the horse. "Taps" (from the Spanish *tapaderas*) are leather shields on the stirrups to protect the feet and to keep them from slipping through the stirrups and getting caught if the rider is thrown. The "malpais" is black volcanic rock. The "cinch" is the strap that holds the saddle on the horse. The "Sam Stack tree" is an old style saddle. The "maguey" is Windy Bill's rope, made of fibers from the maguey plant.

The tune is "Polly Wolly Doodle."

Windy Bill

Words and Music: Anonymous.

Now Wind-y Bill was a Tex-as man and he could rope, you bet, He swore the steer he could-n't tie, he had-n't found him yet. But the boys they knew of an old black steer, sort of an old out-law, That ran down in the mal-pa-is at the foot of a rock-y draw.

Now Windy Bill was a Texas man and he could rope, you bet,
He swore the steer he couldn't tie, he hadn't found him yet.
But the boys they knew of an old black steer, sort of an old outlaw,
That ran down in the malpais at the foot of a rocky draw.

This old black steer had stood his ground, with punchers from everywhere,
And the boys they bet Bill ten to one he couldn't quite get there.
So Bill brought out his old gray horse, withers and back was raw,
Prepared to tackle that big, black brute that ran down in the draw.

With his Brazos bit and his Sam Stack tree and his chaps and taps to boot,
And his old maguey tied hard and fast, Bill swore he'd get that brute.
When old Bill came ridin' around, Blackie began to paw,
Flung his tail up in the air, went a-driftin' down the draw.

The old gray horse went after him, 'cause he'd been eatin' corn,
And Bill he piled his old maguey right around old Blackie's horn.
The old gray horse he stopped right still. The cinches broke like straw.
And the old maguey and the Sam Stack tree went a-driftin' down the draw.

Well Bill he lit in a flint rock pile, his face and hands was scratched,
He said he thought he could rope a snake, but he guessed he'd met his match.
He paid his debts just like a man, without a bit of jaw,
And allowed old Blackie was the boss of anything in the draw.

Now here's the moral to my tale, and that you all must see,
Whenever you go to rope a snake, don't tie him to your tree,
But take your dally welters accordin' to California law,
And you'll never see your old rim fire go a-driftin' down the draw.

California Mode of Catching Cattle

El Cántico del Alba

Mexican Californians created a warm and sociable culture. One delightful tradition was the singing of the morning hymn. When the oldest member of the family awakened he or she would begin singing a hymn. Others would join in, and soon the entire family would be singing. One of the most popular of the morning hymns was "El Cántico del Alba" (the canticle of the dawn).

The words mean:

Now comes the dawn, streaking the day with light. Mary was born to console the sinners, and to light up the sky.

El Cántico del Alba

Words and Music: Anonymous.

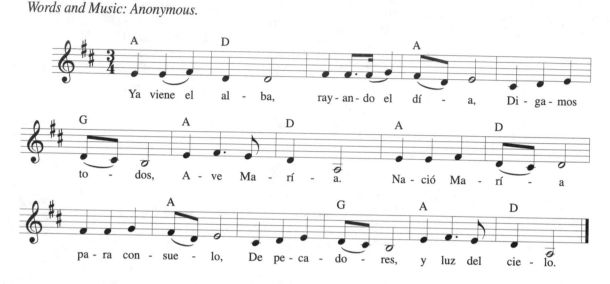

Ya viene el alba, rayando el día,
Digamos todos, Ave María.
Nació María, para consuelo,
De pecadores, y luz del cielo.

Nació María, con eficacia,
Ave María, llena de gracia.
Todos cantemos en alto la voz.
Ave María, Madre de Dios.

La Paloma

Life on the big California ranchos was relaxed. The ranchers worked when necessary, but also enjoyed their leisure time. They raced horses, held bull fights and staged fights between bulls and grizzly bears. The favorite pastime was the *fandango*, a party devoted to socializing, dancing and singing.

La paloma means "the dove." In the song, the dove represents the persona of a soldier in Havana, Cuba. The words tell of his love for a pretty young woman, and of the costs of war. The composer, Sebastian Yradier, had been a soldier stationed in Havana, and he used the Afro-Cuban *habañera* rhythm for his song. "La Paloma" became so popular in Mexico during the mid-19th century that most people believed it had originated there. It has long been a California favorite.

My father, Willard Eugene McNeil, learned this version from ranchers in Pozo, California.

The words mean:

When I left Havana, oh God, no one except myself saw me leave. Now I'm heading for a beautiful place, and she followed me. If a dove comes to your window, treat her kindly, because she is my persona. Share your love, crown her with flowers, she is me. Oh yes, little one, give me your love. Come with me, little one, to where I live. Did I show you the exaggerated drawings of the fortifications from the Austrians? The paper certifies that the war is over.

La Paloma

Words and Music: Sebastian Yradier.

Cuan - do sa - lí de la Ha - ba - na,

vál - ga - me Dios, Na - die

me ha vis - to sa - lir sí no fui yo. Y

u - na lin - da gua - chi - nan - ga a - llá voy yo,

que se vi - no de - trás que mí que sí se - ñor.

Si a tu ven - ta - na lle - ga u - na pa - lo - ma,

Trá - ta - la con ca - ri - ño que es mi per - so - na.

Cuén - ta - le tus a - mor - es bien de mi vi - da

Co - ró - na - la de flo - res que es co - sa mi - a.

Ay chi - ni - ta que sí, Ay que da - me tu a -
mor, Ay que ven - te con - mi - go chi - ni - ta A don - de vi - vo
yo. ¿No te he en - se - ñau no te he en - se - ñau el cua - dri - lá - te - ro
tan di - bu - jau que los aus - tria - cos han - re - ga - lau al a - mo mío tan
de can tau? Y el pa - pe - lí - ti - co cer - ti - fi - cá - ra de que la gue - rra
ha ter - mi - nau, Con tres o - bleas se lo han pe - gau y pe - gau y pe - gau y re - pe - gau.

Cuando salí de la Habana, válgame Dios,
Nadie me ha visto salir sí no fui yo.
Y una linda guachinanga allá voy yo
Que se vino detrás de mí, que sí señor.
Si a tu ventana llega una paloma,
Trátala con cariño que es mi persona.
Cuéntale tus amores bien de mi vida,
Coróna la de flores que es cosa mia.

CHORUS
Ay chinita que sí,
Ay que dame tu amor,
Ay que vente conmigo chinita,
A donde vivo yo.

¿No te he enseñau, no te he enseñau, el cuadrilátero tan dibujau,
Que los austriacos han regalau al amor mío tan decantau?
Y el papelítico certificará de que la guerra ha terminau;
Con tres obleas se lo han pegau, y pegau, y pegau, y repegau.

At a *fandango*, the songs were often sung in couplets, made up spontaneously while the song was being sung. The verses could be in honor of strangers present, to compliment the ladies, or to poke fun at society in general. Sometimes a couplet was begun by a man, and finished by a woman. For example, in 1843, at a *fandango* in Santa Barbara, a Frenchman was in attendance. News had just arrived that American Commodore Thomas Jones had seized Monterey. A man began a couplet to this effect: "If Yankees come the country's lost. There's no one to defend her." A lady quickly replied: "If Frenchmen come, the women folk will willingly surrender!"

All The Way to Californy

Early in 1844, in Nauvoo, Illinois, Joseph Smith, founder and leader of the Church of Latter Day Saints or Mormon Church, instructed his apostles to organize a company and select a location for a settlement in California. Hostility against Mormons was increasing, and they were laying plans for colonies in the west, planning to use them as avenues of escape from Nauvoo if the need arose.

The tune is, "Old Dan Tucker," a popular mid-19th century minstrel song.

All The Way to Californy

Words: Anonymous. Music: Dan Decatur Emmett.

Now in the spring we'll leave Nau-voo, and our jour-ney we'll pur-sue,
Bid the rob-bers all fare-well and let them go to heav-en or hell. So

Chorus
all the way to Cal-i-for-ny, in the spring we'll make our jour-ney,
Pass be-yond the Rock-y Moun-tains, far be-yond the Ar-kan-sas foun-tains.

Now in the spring we'll leave Nauvoo, and our journey we'll pursue,
Bid the robbers all farewell and let them go to heaven or hell.

CHORUS
So all the way to Californy, in the spring we'll make our journey,
Pass beyond the Rocky Mountains, far beyond the Arkansas fountains.

Down on Nauvoo's green grassy plains they burned our houses and our grain,
When they thought we were hell-bent, they asked for aid from the government. CHORUS

Old Governor Ford with a mind so small, has no room for a soul at all,
He neither can be damned or blest if heaven or hell would do its best. CHORUS

The Dying Californian

In June, 1844, Joseph Smith was murdered by a mob. Smith's murder resulted in a mass exodus of Mormons from Nauvoo in 1846. While Mormons in Nauvoo were preparing to cross the Mississippi and make their westward trek across the plains, 238 Mormons living on the East coast, sailed from New York for San Francisco. Led by 26 year old Elder Samuel Brannan, they were hoping to create the new Zion on the shores of California. They sailed on an old weatherbeaten ship called the *Brooklyn*. Their progress was delayed by heavy storms. Food and water supplies ran low, and ten people died at sea.

According to Mormon historian E. Cecil McGavin, "The Dying Californian" was written by a friend of one of the members who died on the *Brooklyn* and was buried at sea.

The Dying Californian

Words and Music: Anonymous.

Lay up nearer, brother nearer, for my limbs are growing cold,
And thy presence seemeth nearer, when thine arms around me fold.
I am dying, brother dying, soon you'll miss me in your berth,
For my form will soon be lying 'neath the ocean's briny surf.

Tell my father when you meet him, that in death I prayed for him,
Prayed that I might some day meet him, in a world that's free from sin.
Tell my mother, God assist her, now that she is growing old,
Say her child would glad have kissed her, as his lips grew pale and cold.

Tell my sister I remember, every kind and parting word,
And my heart has been kept tender, as my thoughts of memory stirred.
Listen brother, closely listen, 'tis my wife I speak of now,
Tell her, tell her how I missed her, when the fever burned my brow.

I am going, brother going, but my hope in God is strong,
I am willing brother knowing that He doeth nothing wrong.
Hark, I hear the Savior speaking, 'tis I know His voice so well,
When I'm gone, oh don't be weeping, brother hear my last farewell.

Elder Brannan's hopes were dashed when Brigham Young decided that Utah's Great Basin was to become the new Zion. Brigham Young did, however, initiate 27 Mormon settlements between the Utah heartland and Los Angeles, California, creating what came to be known as the "Mormon Corridor."

In June, 1846, a month before Brannan's Mormons arrived in San Francisco, a group of Americans invaded the abandoned military post at Sonoma, surrounded Colonel Mariano Guadalupe Vallejo's home, and arrested him as a prisoner of war. They then raised a home-made flag decorated with a grizzly bear, a star, and the words "California Republic." These Americans were unaware that the United States had declared war against Mexico in May. They terminated their California Republic in July, just a month after it was established, when news arrived that Commodore Sloat had captured Monterey and raised the American flag.

When the Mexican War ended, Mexico ceded California, Nevada, Utah, most of Arizona and New Mexico, and parts of Wyoming and Colorado to the United States. Left behind was a sizable Spanish-speaking population of Mexicans and Indians, and an enduring Hispanic culture which continues to influence California.

A Family on the Overland Trail

The Gold Rush

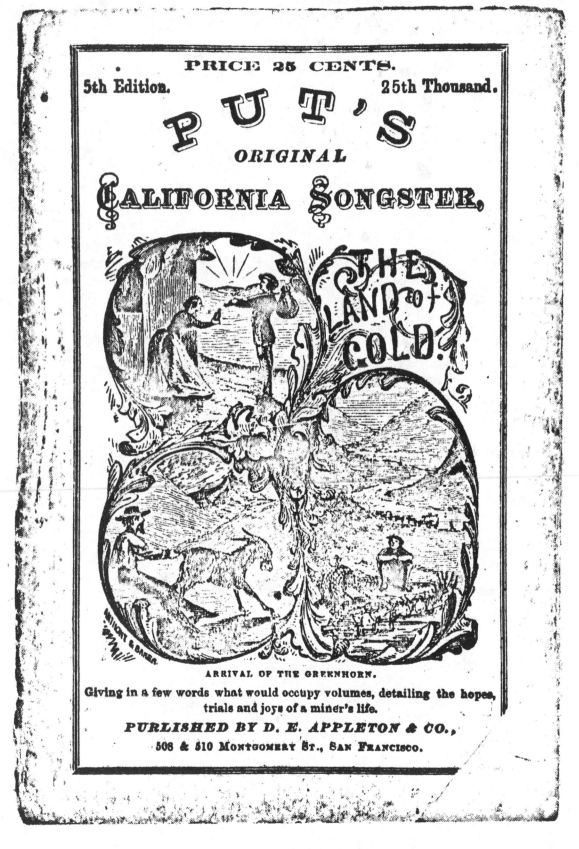

My Darling Clementine

"My Darling Clementine," perhaps the best known of all the California gold rush songs, was written by Percy Montrose a number of years after the gold rush. The song was published in Henry R. Waite's *College Songs* by Oliver Ditson & Company in 1887.

My Darling Clementine

Words and Music: Percy Montrose.

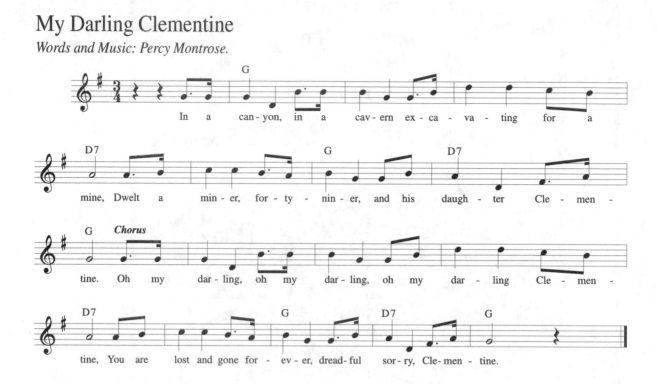

In a canyon, in a cavern, excavating for a mine,
Dwelt a miner, forty-niner, and his daughter Clementine.

Light she was and like a feather, and her shoes were number nine,
Herring boxes without topses, sandals were for Clementine.

CHORUS
Oh my darling, oh my darling, oh my darling Clementine,
You are lost and gone forever, dreadful sorry, Clementine.

Drove she ducklings to the water every morning just at nine,
Stubbed her toe upon a splinter, fell into the foaming brine.

Ruby lips above the water, blowing bubbles soft and fine,
But alas, I was no swimmer, so I lost my Clementine. CHORUS

In a church-yard, near the canyon, where the myrtle doth entwine,
There grow roses, and other posies, fertilized by Clementine.

Then the miner, forty-niner, soon began to peak and pine,
Thought he oughter jine his daughter, now he's with his Clementine. CHORUS

In my dreams she still doth haunt me, robed in garments soaked in brine,
Though in life I used to hug her, now she's dead, I'll draw the line. CHORUS

New verses to "Clementine" continue to appear.

How I missed her, how I missed her, how I missed my Clementine,
So I kissed her little sister, and forgot my Clementine.
Now you scouts should take a lesson from the story of this rhyme,
Mouth-to-mouth resuscitation would have saved my Clementine.

Oh, California

On January 19, 1848, just two weeks before the signing of the peace treaty between Mexico and the United States, James W. Marshall discovered gold at Sutter's Mill in the south fork of the American River. The discovery touched off a wild rush to the California gold fields. Men left families, farms and businesses to search for the precious yellow metal. Ships carried the news to Oregon, Hawaii, Mexico, Chile and Peru. By 1849 one out of every four gold seekers was from a foreign country.

When word finally reached the eastern seaboard, Americans left for California on every available ship. In the two month period from December, 1848 to January, 1849, 178 ships sailed from the East coast around Cape Horn, headed for California, a journey of 18,000 miles that took from five to eight months. The first of the gold rush songs was written by John Nichols in 1848 on board the ship *Eliza*. The song was "Oh, California," a parody of Stephen Foster's newly popular "Oh Susannah."

Oh, California

Words: John Nichols. Music: Stephen Foster.

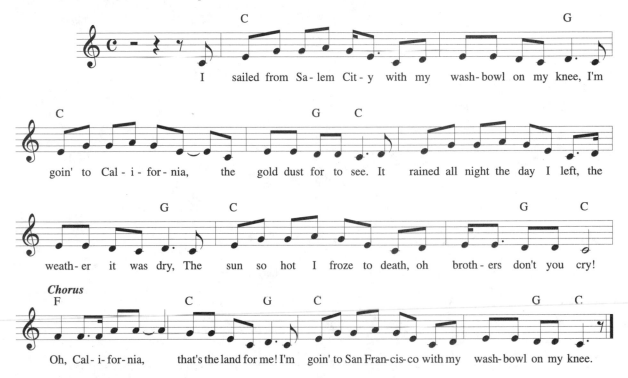

I sailed from Salem City with my washbowl on my knee, I'm goin' to California, the gold dust for to see. It rained all night the day I left, the weather it was dry, The sun so hot I froze to death, oh brothers don't you cry!

Chorus
Oh, California, that's the land for me! I'm goin' to San Francisco with my washbowl on my knee.

I sailed from Salem City with my washbowl on my knee,
I'm goin' to California, the gold dust for to see.
It rained all night the day I left, the weather it was dry,
The sun so hot I froze to death, oh brothers don't you cry!

CHORUS
Oh, California, that's the land for me!
I'm goin' to San Francisco with my washbowl on my knee.

I jumped aboard the '*Liza* ship and traveled on the sea,
And every time I thought of home I wished it wasn't me!
The vessel reared like any horse that had of oats a wealth,
I found it wouldn't throw me, so I thought I'd throw myself! CHORUS

I thought of all the pleasant times we've had together here,
I thought I ought to cry a bit, but couldn't find a tear.
The pilot's bread was in my mouth, the gold dust in my eye,
And though I'm going far away, dear brothers don't you cry! CHORUS

I soon shall be in Frisco, and there I'll look around,
And when I find the gold lumps there I'll pick them off the ground.
I'll scrape the mountains clean, my boys, I'll drain the rivers dry,
A pocketful of rocks bring home, oh brothers don't you cry! CHORUS

Like Argos of the ancient times I'll leave this modern Greece,
I'm bound to California mines to find the golden fleece.
For who would work from morn till night, and live on hog and corn,
When one can pick up there at sight enough to buy a farm. CHORUS

There from the snowy mountain side comes down the golden sand,
And spreads a carpet far and wide o'er all the shining land.
The rivers run on golden beds o'er rocks of golden ore,
The valleys six feet deep are said to hold a plenty more. CHORUS

I'll take my wash-bowl in my hand and thither wend my way,
To wash the gold from out the sand in California.
And when I get my pocket full in that bright land of gold,
I'll have a rich and happy time, live merry till I'm old. CHORUS

A Ripping Trip

Many ships went to Panama, where passengers made their way across the Isthmus, and then waited for ships to transport them up the west coast to California. Advertisements neglected to point out the dangers of crossing the Isthmus, including yellow fever, typhus, malaria and cholera.

Written to the tune of "Pop Goes The Weasel," "A Ripping Trip" was published in *Put's Golden Songster* in 1858.

Chagres River, Isthmus of Panama

A Ripping Trip

Words and Music: Anonymous.

You go a-board of a leak-y boat and sail for San Fran-cis-co, You've got to pump to keep her a-float, you have that, by jin-go. The en-gine soon be-gins to squeak, but nar-y thing to oil her, Im-pos-si-ble to stop the leak, Rip! goes the boil-er.

You go aboard a leaky boat and sail for San Francisco,
You've got to pump to keep her afloat, you have that, by jingo.
The engine soon begins to squeak, but nary thing to oil her.
Impossible to stop the leak, Rip! goes the boiler.

The captain on the promenade lookin' very savage,
The steward and the cabin maid are fightin' about a cabbage.
All about the cabin floor passengers lie seasick,
Steamer's bound to go ashore, Rip! goes the physic!

Pork and beans they can't afford for second cabin passengers,
The cook has tumbled overboard with forty pounds of sassengers,
The engineer, a little tight, braggin' on the Main Line,
Finally gets into a fight, Rip! goes the engine!

Cholera begins to rage, a few have got the scurvy,
Chickens dyin' in their cage, steerage topsy turvy
When you get to Panama, boatmen want a back-load,
Officers begin to jaw, Rip! goes the railroad!

When home you'll tell an awful tale and always will be thinkin',
How long you had to pump and bail to keep the tub from sinkin'.
Of course you'll take a glass of gin, 'Twill make you feel so funny,
Some city sharp will rope you in, Rip! goes your money!

Seeing the Elephant

The first gold rush song written on California soil was "Seeing The Elephant," by David G. Robinson, a New England roadshow trouper, who established one of the first theatrical houses in San Francisco. "Seeing The Elephant" was the title song of Robinson's first play, which was a local version of a popular eastern satire on the gold rush. The song was published in *Comic Songs; or Hits at San Francisco* in 1853. John Stone also included it in his *Put's Original California Songster* in 1855.

The 19th century expression "Seeing the Elephant" meant: "When a man is disappointed in anything he undertakes, when he has seen enough, when he gets sick and tired of any job he may have set himself about, he has seen the elephant." (From Kendall's *Santa Fe Expedition*, 1844)

Seeing the Elephant

Words: David G. Robinson. Music: Dan Decatur Emmett.

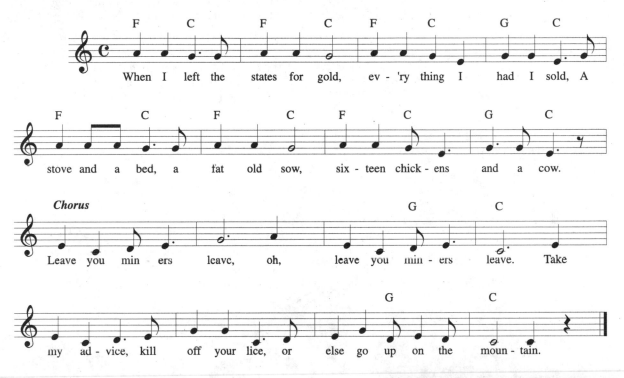

When I left the states for gold, ev-'ry thing I had I sold, A stove and a bed, a fat old sow, six-teen chick-ens and a cow.

Chorus

Leave you min ers leave, oh, leave you min-ers leave. Take my ad-vice, kill off your lice, or else go up on the moun-tain.

When I left the states for gold, everything I had I sold,
A stove and a bed, a fat old sow, sixteen chickens and a cow.

CHORUS
Leave you miners leave, oh leave you miners leave.
Take my advice, kill off your lice, or else go up on the mountain.

Being brave I cut and carved, on the desert nearly starved,
My old mule laid down and died, I had no blanket so I took his hide. CHORUS

The poor coyote stole my meat, so I had naught but bread to eat,
It was not long till that gave out, then how I cursed the Truckee route! CHORUS

Because I would not pay my bill they kicked me out of Downieville,
I stole a mule and lost the trail, and then fetched up in Hangtown Jail. CHORUS

Canvas roof and paper walls, twenty horse thieves in the stalls,
I did as I had done before, coyoted out from beneath the floor. CHORUS

The people threatened hard my life because I stole a miner's wife,
They showed me a rope to give me sign, then off I went to the southern mines. CHORUS

I fell in love with a California girl, her eyes were gray and her hair did curl,
Her nose turned up to get rid of her chin, says she, "You're a miner, you can't come in." CHORUS

When the elephant I had seen I'm damned if I thought I was green,
And others say, both night and morn, they saw him comin' round the Horn. CHORUS

Avalanche in the Sierra Nevada Mountains

Crossing the Plains

In the first two years of the gold rush, California's non-Indian population grew from 30,000 to 200,000. Emigrants gathered in April and May at Independence, Westport and St. Joseph, Missouri to join wagon trains. The covered wagons were mostly Conestoga wagons manufactured in the east, and were soon nicknamed "prairie schooners." A typical load for each adult included 200 pounds of flour, 30 pounds of pilot bread, 75 pounds of bacon, 25 pounds of sugar, plus rice, coffee, tea and beans. Teams were made up of ten to twelve horses or mules, or twelve oxen. Here's an excerpt from the diary of a forty-niner:

May third, 1849. Fifteen miles to Bull Creek. The guide pointed out the continuous rise and fall of the track across what are rightly called the billows, or little ridges of the prairie. "No, it's not high mountains ner great rivers ner hostile injuns," says Meek, "that'll give us most grief. It's the long grind o' doin' every day's work reglar an' not let-up fer nothin'. Figger it out fur yourself; two thousand one hundred miles - four months to do it in between April rains and September snows - 123 days. How much a day and every cussed day?"

I saw the point. Seventeen miles a day.

"Yaas" drawled the scout. "And every day rain, hail, cholera, breakdowns, lame mules, sick cows, washouts, prairie fires, flooded coulees, lost horses, dust storms and alkalai water. Seventeen miles every day or you land in the snow and eat each other like the Donner party done in '46."

May 13, 1849. Long pull. Here we are beginning to meet people who are turning back, discouraged. They had seen enough of the elephant. Graves are more frequent these last days. We saw whitening on the plains, bones of animals which had died on the way. (From Archer Butler Hulbert's *'49ers*, 1931)

"Crossing The Plains" was another of Old Put's classics from *Put's Original California Songster*, first published in 1855. Five editions of the songster were published by D. E. Appleton & Co. between 1855 and 1870, selling twenty-five thousand copies.

Crossing the Plains

Crossing the Plains

Words: John A. Stone. Music: Anonymous.

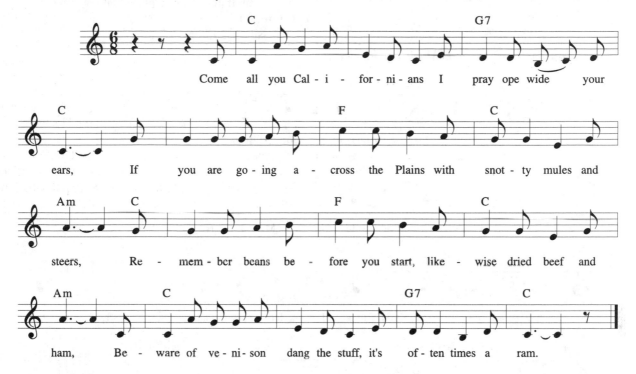

Come all you Cal-i-for-ni-ans I pray ope wide your ears, If you are go-ing a-cross the Plains with snot-ty mules and steers, Re-mem-ber beans be-fore you start, like-wise dried beef and ham, Be-ware of ve-ni-son dang the stuff, it's of-ten times a ram.

Come all you Californians I pray ope wide your ears,
If you are going across the Plains with snotty mules and steers,
Remember beans before you start, likewise dried beef and ham,
Beware of venison, dang the stuff, it's often times a ram.

You must buy two revolvers, a bowie knife and belt,
Says you, "Old feller, now stand off, or I will have your pelt."
The greenhorn looks around about, but not a soul can see,
Says he, "There's not a man in town, but what's afraid of me."

Don't shave your beard but cultivate your down and let it grow.
And when you do return 'twill be as soft and white as snow,
Your lovely Jane will be surprised, your ma'll begin to cook,
The greenhorn to his mother'll say, "How savage I must look!"

"How do you like it overland?" his mother she will say,
"All right, excepting cooking, then the devil is to pay,
For some won't cook, and others can't, and then it's curse and damn,
The coffee pot's begun to leak, so has the frying pan."

You calculate on sixty days to take you over the Plains,
But when you lack for bread and beef, for coffee and for brains,
Your sixty days are a hundred or more, your grub you've got to divide,
Your steers and mules are alkalied, so foot it you cannot ride.

You have to stand a watch at night to keep the Indians off,
About sundown some heads will ache, and some begin to cough,
To be deprived of health we know is always very hard,
But every night someone is sick to get rid of standing guard.

Your canteens they should be well filled, with poison alkali,
So when you get tired of traveling, you can cramp right up and die.
The best thing in the world to keep your bowels loose and free
Is fight and quarrel among yourselves, and seldom if ever agree.

There's not a log to make a seat, along the river Platte,
So when you eat you've got to stand, or set down square and flat,
It's fun to cook with buffalo wood, take some that's newly born,
If I knew then what I know now, I'd of gone around the horn.

The desert's nearly death on corns, while walking in the sand,
And drive a jackass by the tail, it's damn this overland,
I'd rather ride a raft at sea, and then at once be lost,
Says Bill, "Let's leave this poor old mule, we can't get him across."

The ladies have the hardest time, when they emigrate by land,
And when they cook with buffalo wood, they often burn a hand,
And then they jaw their husbands round, get mad and spill the tea,
I wish to God they'd be taken down with a turn of di-a-ree.

When you arrive at Placerville, or Sacramento City,
You haven't a cent to buy a meal, no money, what a pity,
Your striped pants are all wore out which causes people to laugh,
To see you gaping round the town like a great big brindle calf.

You're lazy, poor, and all broke down, such hardships you endure,
The post office at Sacramento all such men will cure,
You'll find a line from ma and pa, and one from lovely Sal,
If that don't physic you every mail, you never will get well.

Joe Bowers

One of the most popular of all the gold rush songs was "Joe Bowers." Just after striking it rich, Joe learns that his beloved Sally has married another man. John Woodward, who wrote the words, was a popular minstrel entertainer.

This version was passed down through my family from my great-grandfather Cary Calvin Oakley, who arrived in the California goldfields in 1850. He sang it to the same tune as "Crossing the Plains."

Joe Bowers

Words: John Woodward. Music: Anonymous.

My name it is Joe Bow-ers, I have a broth-er Ike. I come from old Mis-sou-ri, yes all the way from Pike, I'll tell you how I left there, and why I come to roam, And leave my dear old Mam-my, so far a-way from home.

My name it is Joe Bowers, I have a brother Ike.
I come from old Missouri, yes all the way from Pike,
I'll tell you how I left there, why I come to roam,
And leave my dear old mammy, so far away from home.

I used to love a gal there, her name was Sally Black,
I asked her to marry me, she said it was a whack.
Says she to me, "Joe Bowers, before we hitch for life,
You oughtta have a little house to keep a little wife."

Says I to her, "Dear Sally, dear Sally for your sake,
I'll go to California and try to raise a stake."
Says she to me, "Joe Bowers, you are the chap to win!"
She give me a kiss to seal the bargain, and she throwed a dozen in.

I'll ne'er forget my feelings when I bid adieu to all.
Sally cotched me round the neck and I began to bawl,
When I sot in they all commenced, you never saw the like,
How they took down and cried, the day I left old Pike.

When I got to this here country, I hadn't nary red.
I had such wolfish feelings I wished myself most dead,
I worked both late and early, through rain and sun and snow,
I was workin' for my Sally, so 'twas all the same to Joe.

And then I made a lucky strike, as the gold itself did tell,
I was workin' for my Sally, the gal I loved so well,
But then I got a letter from my dear kind brother Ike,
It came from old Missouri, yes all the way from Pike.

It said my Sal was fickle, her love for me had fled.
She'd gone and married a butcher whose hair was awful red,
It told me more than that, it's enough to make me swear,
Said Sally had a baby, and the baby had red hair!

California Prospector

The Days of Forty-Nine

Life in the mining camps was not easy. The work was hard, the food terrible, and sleeping accommodations uncomfortable. After a grueling day's work, the evening was usually taken up with heavy drinking and gambling. The combination of homesickness, mixed ethnic and racial groups, heavy drinking and gambling resulted in frequent fights and killings.

Charley Rhoades's "The Days Of Forty-Nine" entered the oral tradition early, and has many versions and verses, a few of which are printed here.

The Days of Forty-Nine

Words: Charley Rhoades. Music: Anonymous.

I'm old Tom Moore, a bummer sure, of the good old golden days, They call me a bummer and a gin sot too, but what care I for praise, I wander around from town to town just like a ramble-in' sign, And the people all say, "There goes Tom Moore, of the days of forty-nine." In the days of old, in the days of gold, how oft-times I re-pine, In the days of old when we dug up the gold, in the days of forty-nine.

I'm old Tom Moore, a bummer sure, of the good old golden days,
They call me a bummer and a gin sot too, but what care I for praise,
I wander around from town to town, just like a ramblin' sign,
And the people all say, "There goes Tom Moore, of the days of forty-nine."

CHORUS
In the days of old, in the days of gold, how oft-times I repine,
In the days of old when we dug up the gold, in the days of forty-nine.

My comrades they all knew me well, a jolly, saucy crew,
A few hard-cases I will admit, though they were brave and true,
Whatever the pinch they never would flinch, they never would fret or whine,
Like good old bricks they stood the kicks in the days of forty-nine.

There was old lame Jess, a hard old cuss, he never did repent,
He was never known to miss a drink, or ever spend a cent.
But old lame Jess, like all the rest, to death he did resign,
And in his bloom went up the flume in the days of forty-nine. CHORUS

There was New York Jake, the butcher's boy, he was always gettin' tight,
And every time that he'd get full he was lookin' for a fight.
Then Jake rampaged against a knife in the hands of old Bob Sine,
And over Jake we held a wake in the days of forty-nine.

There was ragshag Bill from Buffalo, I never will forget.
He would roar all day and he'd roar all night, and I guess he's roarin' yet.
One night Bill fell in a prospect hole in a roarin' bad design,
And in that hole Bill roared out his soul in the days of forty-nine. CHORUS

There was Kentuck Bill, one of the boys who was always in the game,
No matter whether he lost or won, to him it was all the same,
He'd ante a slug, he'd pass the buck, he'd go for a hat full blind,
In the game of death, Bill lost his breath in the days of forty-nine.

There was Monte Pete, I'll ne'er forget the luck he always had,
He'd deal for you both night and day, or as long as you had a scad,
One night a pistol laid him out, 'twas his last lay out in fine,
It caught Pete sure, right bang at the door, in the days of forty-nine.
CHORUS

There was another chap from New Orleans, Big Reuben was his name,
On the plaza there with a sardine box he opened a faro game,
He dealt so fair that a millionaire he became in course of time,
Till death stepped in and called the turn in the days of forty-nine.

Of all the comrades that I've had there's none that's left to boast,
And I'm left alone in my misery like some poor wanderin' ghost.
And as I roam from town to town, they call me the ramblin' sign,
There goes Tom Moore, a bummer sure, of the days of forty-nine.
CHORUS

Using the same tune, J. Riley Mains wrote a popular follow-up song called "The Good Old Days Of '50, '1 And '2," which begins:

Tom Moore has sung of '49, and the pioneers who came
Across the plains and 'round the horn in search of gold and fame,
But in his song he tells us not one word of those we knew,
Those pioneers of the good old days of '50, '1 and '2.

Cripple Creek

Despite these difficult conditions, the miners would often organize a dance, which usually lasted all night. When there were no women present in the camp, the miners danced with each other. Every man who wore a white patch on his pants was considered a lady. The caller improvised to suit the situation.

The traditional southern banjo tune "Cripple Creek" is still a favorite among square dancers.

No Ladies at the Dance

Cripple Creek

Music: Anonymous.

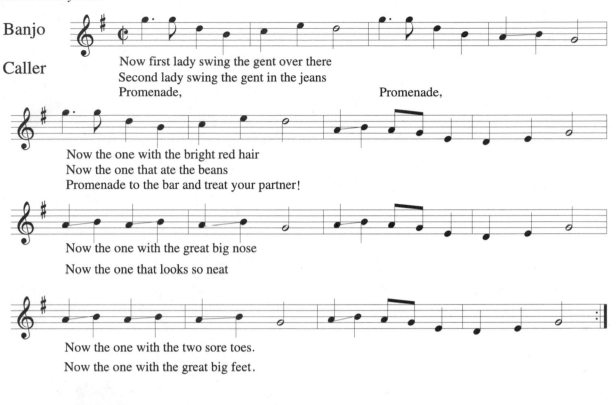

Banjo

Caller
Now first lady swing the gent over there
Second lady swing the gent in the jeans
Promenade,   Promenade,

Now the one with the bright red hair
Now the one that ate the beans
Promenade to the bar and treat your partner!

Now the one with the great big nose

Now the one that looks so neat

Now the one with the two sore toes.

Now the one with the great big feet.

Caller: Now first lady swing the gent over there
And now the one with the bright red hair
Now the one with the great big nose
And now the one with two sore toes.

Second lady swing the gent in the jeans
And now the one that ate the beans
And now the one that looks so neat
And now the one with the great big feet.

Promenade, promenade,
Promenade to the bar and treat your partner!

California Ball

In mining communities where there were women present, every female attended the dances, regardless of age, ethnicity, occupation, reputation or marital status.

"Old Put" set his words to the tune of R. P. Buckley's ever popular song "Wait For The Wagon."

California Ball

Words: John A. Stone. Music: R. P. Buckley.

The la-dies through the dig-gings wind, and o-ver moun-tains tall, With young ones tag-ging on be-hind flat-foot-ed for the ball. The man-a-ger be-gins to curse and swag-gers through the hall, For moth-ers they've gone out to nurse their ba-bies at the ball.

Chorus

Wait for the mu-sic! Wait for the mu-sic! Wait for the mu-sic! And we'll all have a dance!

The ladies through the diggings wind, and over mountains tall,
With young ones tagging on behind flat-footed for the ball.
The manager begins to curse and swaggers through the hall,
For mothers they've gone out to nurse their babies at the ball.

CHORUS
Wait for the music! Wait for the music!
Wait for the music! And we'll all have a dance!

'Twould make our eastern people cave, to see the great and small,
The old, with one foot in the grave, all splurging at a ball.
A dozen babies on the bed and all begin to squall,
The mothers wish the brats were dead, for crying at the ball! CHORUS

Old women in their bloomer rigs are fond of "balance all."
And "weighty" when it comes to jigs, and so on, at the ball!

A yearling miss fills out the set, although not very tall,
"I'm anxious now," she says, "you bet, to proceed with the ball!" CHORUS

A married woman, gentle dove, with nary tooth at all,
Sits in the corner making love with a stranger at the ball!
The Spanish hags of ill repute for brandy loudly call,
And no one dares their right dispute to freedom at the ball! CHORUS

A drunken loafer at the dance informs them one and all,
With bowie knife stuck in his pants, "The best man at the ball!"
The gambler all the money wins, to bed the drunkest crawl,
And fighting then of course begins with rowdies at the ball! CHORUS

They rush it like a railroad car and often is the call
Of "Promenade up to the bar!" for whiskey at the ball!
"Old Alky" makes their bowels yearn, they stagger round and fall,
And ladies say when they return, "Oh, what a splendid ball!" CHORUS

Sweet Betsey from Pike

The women who traveled to California in the 1840s and '50s shared in the hardships of the journey. One of the most popular songs written and sung during the gold rush was "Sweet Betsey [sic] from Pike." The tune was originally "Villikens And His Dinah," an English music hall song composed by John Parry. The tune has dozens of parodies in England, Ireland and the United States.

"Sweet Betsey" was published in *Put's Golden Songster*. I learned this version from my great- uncle James Asa "Ace" Oakley, a California cattle rancher.

The reference to Brigham Young in the song is reflective of the prejudices common in California during the gold rush era. In addition to Mormons, the targets also included Indians, Mexicans, Chinese, Central Americans, South Sea Islanders and African-Americans.

Sweet Betsey from Pike

Words: John A. Stone. Music: John Parry.

Oh don't you re - mem - ber sweet Bet - sey from Pike, Who crossed the high moun - tains with her lov - er Ike, With one yoke of ox - en, one spot - ted hog, A tall Shang - hai roos - ter and a big yel - la dog.

Oh don't you remember sweet Betsey from Pike,
Who crossed the high mountains with her lover Ike,
With one yoke of oxen, one spotted hog,
A tall Shanghai rooster and a big yella dog.

One evenin' quite early they camped on the Platte,
'Twas nearby the road on a green shady flat,
Sweet Betsey grew weary, lay down to repose,
While Isaac stood gazin' at his Pike County rose.

They soon reached the desert where Betsey gave out;
Down in the sand she lay rollin' about,
While Ike with great wonder looked on in surprise, sayin'
"Betsey, get up, you'll get sand in your eyes!"

They stopped at Salt Lake to inquire the way,
And Brigham he swore that Sweet Betsey should stay,

Sweet Betsey got scairt and she run like a deer
While Brigham stood pawin' the ground like a steer.

The Injuns come down in a wild yellin' horde,
And Betsey was scairt they would scalp her adored,
So behind the front wagon wheel Betsey did crawl,
And there she fought Injuns with musket and ball.

The horses ran off and the cattle all died,
The last piece of bacon that mornin' was fried,
Poor Ike got discouraged, Betsey got mad,
The dog wagged his tail and looked wonderfully sad.

They climbed to the top of a very high hill,
And they stood lookin' down upon old Placerville,
Ike shouted and said as he cast his eyes down,
"Sweet Betsey, my darlin', we've got to Hangtown."

John Chinaman's Appeal

The gold rush attracted many immigrants from China. Early California governors encouraged Chinese immigration, referring to the Chinese as "one of the most worthy classes of our newly adopted citizens." The white miners, however, wanted California's gold for themselves, and the state's attitude toward the new Chinese immigrants changed quickly from welcome to hostility.

Here is an abridged version of a satirical article by Mark Twain called *The Disgraceful Persecution of a Boy*. Twain wrote it in 1864 for the *Morning Call*, a San Francisco newspaper. The editor refused to print it. He told Twain that the paper was "the washerwoman's paper," supported by the poor, that the poor were Irish, and that the Irish hated the Chinese. He said without them the newspaper would not last a month.

The article was finally published by Harper and Brothers in 1875, along with a number of Mark Twain's other previously unpublished works.

In San Francisco the other day, "A well-dressed boy on his way to Sunday school was arrested and thrown into the city prison for stoning Chinamen...."

Before we side against him, let us give him a chance. Let us hear the testimony for the defense. He was a well-dressed boy, and a Sunday school scholar, and therefore the chances are that his parents were intelligent, well-to-do people with just enough natural villainy in their composition to make them yearn after the daily papers, and enjoy them. And so this boy had opportunities to learn all through the week how to do right, as well as on Sunday. It was in this way that he found out that the great commonwealth of California imposes an unlawful mining tax upon John, the foreigner, and allows Patrick, the foreigner, to dig gold for nothing. It was in this way that he found out that a respectable number of the tax-gatherers, it would be unkind to say all of them, collect the tax twice instead of once. And that, inasmuch as they do it solely to discourage Chinese immigration into the mines, it is a thing that is much applauded.

It was in this way that he found out that when a white man robs a sluice box they make him leave the camp, and when a Chinaman does that thing, they hang him...

Lunchtime at the Long Tom

It was in this way that the boy found out that a Chinaman had no rights that any man was bound to respect. That he had no sorrows that any man was bound to pity. That neither his life nor his liberty was worth the purchase of a penny when a white man needed a scapegoat. That nobody loved Chinamen, nobody befriended them, nobody spared them suffering when it was convenient to inflict it. Everybody, individuals, communities, the majesty of the state itself joined in hating, abusing and persecuting these humble strangers.

And therefore, what could have been more natural than for this sunny-hearted boy, tripping along to Sunday school, with his mind teeming with freshly learned incentives to high and virtuous action, to say to himself, "Ah, there goes a Chinaman. God will not love me if I do not stone him..."

Chinese in San Francisco

"John Chinaman's Appeal," sung to the tune "Yankee Doodle," was a remarkably sympathetic song for the period. Nearly every other gold rush song that mentioned the Chinese reflected a negative attitude. The song also accurately incorporated a number of historical events experienced by Chinese miners.

Mart Taylor, the composer, was a minstrel show performer. His troupe was called "Taylor's Original Minstrel Company." Like other California minstrels, he wrote a number of gold rush songs and published them in his book *The Gold Diggers' Songbook*, in 1856.

The "long tom" in the song is a sluice box, measuring in length between 18 and 50 feet. It is used to separate the gold from sand and gravel. The "rocker" is a box on rockers. The rocking motion of the box agitates the sluice, separating the gold. The "cue"[sic] is the pigtail worn by the Chinese miners.

John Chinaman's Appeal

Words: Mart Taylor. Music: Anonymous.

American, now mind my song, if you would but hear me sing,
And I will tell you of the wrong that happened unto Gee Sing.
In fifty-two I left my home and bid farewell to Hong Kong,
And started with Cup Gee to roam, to the land where they use the "long tom."

In forty days I reached the bay, and nearly starved was I, sir,
I cooked and ate a dog one day, I did not know the laws, sir.
But soon I found my dainty meal was 'gainst the city order,
The penalty I had to feel, confound the old Recorder.

By paying up my costs and fines they freed me from the locker,
And then I started for the mines, I got a pick and rocker.
I went to work in an untouched place, I'm sure I meant no blame, sir,
But a white man struck me in the face and told me to leave his claim, sir.

'Twas then I packed my tools away and set up in a new place,
But there they would not let me stay, they did not like the *cue* race.
And then I knew not what to do, I could not get employ,
The Know Nothings would bid me go, *'twas tu nah mug ahoy.*

I started then for Weaverville where Chinamen were thriving,
But found our China agents there in ancient feuds were driving.
So I pitched into politics, but with the weaker party,
The Cantons with their clubs and bricks did drub us out right hearty.

I started for Yreka then, I thought that I would stay there,
But found for even Chinamen the diggings would not pay there.
So I set up a washing shop, but how extremely funny,
The miners all had dirty clothes, but not a cent of money.

I met a big stout Indian once, he stopped me on the trail, sir,
He drew an awful scalping knife and I trembled for my tail, sir.
He caught me by the hair, it's true, in a manner quite uncivil,
But when he saw my awful cue, he thought I was the devil.

Oh, now my friends I'm going away from this infernal place, sir,
The balance of my days I'll spend with the celestial race, sir.
I'll go to raising rice and tea, I'll be a heathen ever,
For Christians all have treated me as men should be used never.

We're All A-Panning

California's first constitutional convention met on September 1, 1849. Many of the delegates did not speak English, so the translators kept very busy. The more emotional subjects included slavery, gambling, a state lottery and allowing non-whites the vote, all of which were rejected. They established the state boundaries, voted to publish laws in both English and Spanish, and agreed to locate the seat of government in San Jose. One year later, on September 9, 1850, President Millard Fillmore signed the bill, and California became the 31st state in the Union. Many immigrants to the new state quickly discovered that there were easier ways than mining to get their hands on California's gold.

The tune is "We're A' Noddin'," from Scotland. The song was published in Taylor's *The Gold Diggers' Songbook* in 1856.

We're All A-Panning

Words: Mart Taylor. Music: Anonymous.

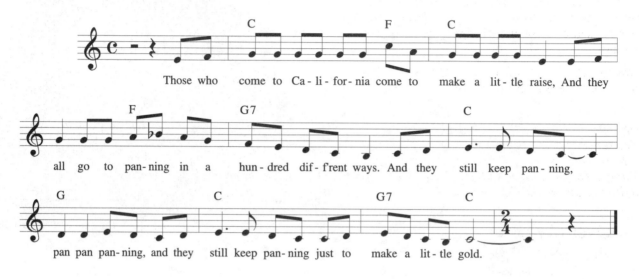

Those who come to California come to make a little raise, And they all go to panning in a hundred diff'rent ways. And they still keep panning, pan pan panning, and they still keep panning just to make a little gold.

Those who come to California come to make a little raise,
And they all go to panning in a hundred different ways.
And they still keep panning, pan pan panning,
And they still keep panning just to make a little gold.

The merchant shows his article and urges you to buy,
And he says they cost him dearly, but "it's all in your eye."
This is *his* way of panning, pan pan panning,
This is his way of panning just to get a little gold.

And the crazy politician all his enemies will curse,
While he seeks to get his fingers in the heavy public purse.
'Tis a *tricky* way of panning, pan pan panning,
'Tis a tricky way of panning just to get a little gold.

The preacher keeps a preaching, going everywhere it pays,
He bestows the greatest blessings where he makes the biggest raise.
'Tis a *pious* way of panning, pan pan panning,
'Tis a pious way of panning just to get a little gold.

The attorney all his knowledge of the statutes will reveal,
And you'd think him talking truly when he's lying like the devil.
'Tis a *wicked* way of panning, pan pan panning,
'Tis a wicked way of panning just to get a little gold.

There's the gambler has his cappers who are looking all about,
And when they can find a sucker they are sure to pan him out.
'Tis a *thieving* way of panning, pan pan panning,
'Tis a thieving way of panning just to get a little gold.

And the robber comes upon you with a pistol or a knife,
And declares he'll have your money or he's bound to take your life.
'Tis a *horrid* way of panning, pan pan panning,
'Tis a horrid way of panning just to get a little gold.

But the miner in his diggings keeps a-panning all the while,
And he's ever well contented when he's adding to his pile.
'Tis an *honest* way of panning, pan pan panning,
'Tis an honest way of panning just to make a little raise.

Over My Head

The African-Americans who came to California during the gold rush comprised about one percent of the state's non-Indian population. Lured by the promise of riches in the gold fields, more than a thousand mined for gold, and some became wealthy. Others worked in the cities as stewards, cooks and bootblacks; some started businesses, including clothing stores, boarding houses, boot manufacturing companies, livery stables, saloons, barber shops and bath houses. California's African-Americans were for the most part much better off financially than blacks in other states.

While the majority came to California of their own free will, many came as slaves. When Peter Lester, a black abolitionist from Philadelphia, arrived in San Francisco, he was surprised to find slavery existing in a free state. Lester invited many slaves to his home, lectured them on their rights, and taught them anti-slavery songs.

This traditional African-American song was revived during the civil rights movement of the 1960s.

African-American James P. Beckwourth, gold miner, trapper, pathfinder and U.S. Army scout, discovered Beckwourth Pass through the Sierra Nevada mountains, and led the first wagon train through the pass. General Kearny solicited Beckwourth's assistance during the California Bear Flag Rebellion.

Over My Head

Words and Music: Anonymous.

Over my head, I feel freedom in the air,
Over my head, I feel freedom in the air,
Over my head, I feel freedom in the air,
There must be a God somewhere.

Over my head, I feel victory in the air,
Over my head, I feel victory in the air,
Over my head, I feel victory in the air,
There must be a God somewhere.

Noah

The social center for California African-Americans was the church. The first black church was an African Methodist Episcopal church, organized in 1850 in Sacramento. San Francisco's first black churches were A.M.E. and Baptist, both organized in 1852. These two denominations dominated black religious activities in California throughout the 1850s and '60s, and brought new musical sounds to California.

Noah is a traditional African-American religious song.

Noah

Words and Music: Anonymous.

Well it's-a oh, No - ah, my Lord-y Oh,

oh No - ah, Mmm high, oh No - ah, God's gon - na ride on the

rain - in' tide, gon - na ride on the rain - in' tide.

Said He's gon - na ride on the rain - in' tide.

Child - ren stop, still, lis - ten to me, God walked down by the

bri - ny sea. De - clared the e - vil, sins of man, De - clared that - a He would des -

troy the land. God called No - ah, No - ah stopped, He said, "No - ah I want you to

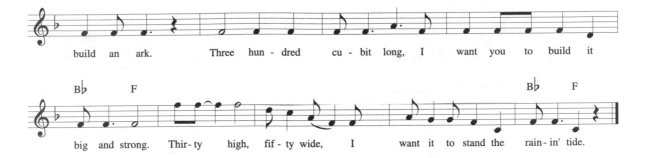

build an ark. Three hun-dred cu-bit long, I want you to build it

big and strong. Thir-ty high, fif-ty wide, I want it to stand the rain-in' tide.

Well it's oh, Noah, my Lordy oh, oh Noah,
Mm high, oh Noah, God's gonna ride on the rainin' tide,
God's gonna ride on the rainin' tide,
Said he's gonna ride on the rainin' tide.

Children stop, still, listen to me,
God walked down by the briny sea,
Declared the evil, sins of man,
Declared that He would destroy the land.
God called Noah, Noah stopped,
He said, "Noah I want you to build an Ark,
Three hundred cubit long,
I want you to build it big and strong.
Thirty high, fifty wide,
I want it to stand the rainin' tide."

Well it's oh, oh Noah, my Lordy oh, oh Noah
Mm high, oh Noah, God's gonna ride on the rainin' tide.
Brother Noah, hear God talkin'
Said He gonna ride on the rainin' tide.

Well, after God told Noah what to do,
Noah began to cut and hew,

Ringin' of the hammer of judgement
To bring another song, sinner repent.
God called the animals two by two
He called the ox, the camel, the kangaroo.
Then He called Jacob, Shem and Ham,
Then God began to destroy the land.
Shook the mountains, stirred the sea,
And then He hitched the wind to the chariot wheel.

Stood on land, stepped off the shore
Declared that time gonna be no more

Oh, oh Noah, my Lordy oh, oh Noah,
Mm High, oh Noah, God's gonna ride on the rainin' tide.
Brother Noah, hear God talkin'
Said he's gonna ride on the rainin' tide.

North to Victoria

Despite their relative affluence, life was difficult for black Californians. They paid their taxes but were not allowed to vote, they could not testify in court against white men who committed crimes against them, and there were no provisions for financing the education of minority children.

In 1858, the state legislature introduced and nearly passed the Warfield bill, an anti-Negro immigration bill which included a provision that blacks would be required to carry proof of their residence with them at all times. Those found without their papers would be forced into a type of slavery for six months until they could earn enough money to pay for their passage out of the state. During this same period, gold was discovered on the Fraser River in British Columbia, and Canadians were urging California's black citizens to emigrate to Victoria. Angry with the state legislature's continued racist actions, about fifteen percent of California's African-American population left for Canada. They were accepted into Canada's white churches and schools, they bought land, found jobs, opened businesses and mined gold. Hundreds became Canadian citizens.

"North To Victoria" was originally a poem, written in 1858 by a black Californian named Priscilla Stewart.

PROCEEDINGS

OF THE

SECOND ANNUAL CONVENTION

OF THE

COLORED CITIZENS

OF THE

State of California.

HELD IN THE CITY OF SACRAMENTO, DEC. 9TH, 10TH, 11TH, AND 12TH.

SAN FRANCISCO:
J. H. UDELL AND W. RANDALL, PRINTERS.
1856.

North to Victoria

Words: Priscilla Stewart. Music: Anonymous.

God bless the queen's maj-es-ty, God bless the queen's maj-es-ty, God bless the queen's maj-es-ty, Her scep-ter and her throne, She looked on us with sym-pa-thy, She looked on us with sym-pa-thy, She looked on us with sym-pa-thy, And of-fered us a home.

God bless the Queen's majesty,
God bless the Queen's majesty,
God bless the Queen's majesty,
Her scepter and her throne.
She looked on us with sympathy,
She looked on us with sympathy,
She looked on us with sympathy
And offered us a home.

Far better to breathe Canadian air,
Better to breathe Canadian air,
Better to breathe Canadian air
Where all are free and well,
Than live in slavery's atmosphere,
Live in slavery's atmosphere,
Live in slavery's atmosphere
And wear the chains of hell!

The June 20, 1857 edition of the Northern California African-American newspaper *The Mirror of the Times* published the poem "*Turncoat A. and Treacherous T.*," author unknown, which ridiculed those who would remain in California.

While turn-coat A., and treacherous T.,
Urge on non-emigration,
Say to all nations, kindreds and tongues,
"Farewell expatriation -
We have not courage - spunk enough
To think of emigration.

We'll rather be as Southern slaves,
Bound here by BLACK taxation;
Than have a puny Cole to rule,
Or speak on emigration.
To Mexico we will not go
Nor Moore's Canadian station."

The reference to "BLACK taxation" was that although California blacks were not allowed to vote, they were required to pay a poll tax. The reference about going to Mexico was to a group that proposed emigrating to Sonora, Mexico.

Steam Navigation Thieves

California's waterways, especially San Francisco Bay, the Sacramento River, the Feather River and the San Joaquin River, provided convenient transportation routes. By the end of 1850, thirty steamboats were hauling goods and passengers between San Francisco and Marysville. In February, 1854, some of the steamboat owners combined to organize The California Steam Navigation Company. For the next fifteen years, the company had a monopoly on freight and passenger service between San Francisco and the main inland ports. Their rates were exorbitant, but when smaller companies attempted to compete, company boats forced the competitors' boats onto sandbars, or rammed them midstream.

The melody is "Walk Ye In," a 19th century minstrel song.

Steam Navigation Thieves

Words: John A. Stone. Music: Anonymous

The only legal swindle which the people cannot sever,
Is the steamboat imposition on the Sacramento River,
It would surely be a blessing if the company would fail,
And if another organizes, ride them on a rail.

CHORUS
Remember now! remember now! remember what I say,
Keep your hands upon your money, or they'll rob you on the way,
If you don't believe it, try it, either to or from the Bay.

When you start from Sacramento and get stuck upon the sand,
All you have to do is jump ashore and foot it up by land.
They have robbed a world of people, still there's none that say a word,
For if ever they were passengers, they'd be thrown overboard. CHORUS

Sacramento

In the 1850s, whaling activity was shifting from the Atlantic Ocean to the Pacific, and San Francisco became the major whaling port. In 1855, five hundred whaling ships visited the Pacific coast, and the California gold fields became the subject of some of the sailors' sea chanteys.

The tune is "The Camptown Races," one of Stephen Foster's most popular minstrel songs. Some of the words to the chorus of "Sacramento" came from the song "Ho! For California," written by Jesse Hutchinson of the famous Hutchinson family, best known for their anti-slavery songs. Jesse's song, published in 1851, said:

Then, ho, brothers, ho, to California go,
No slave shall toil on God's free soil,
On the banks of the Sacramento.
Heigh O, and away we go,
Chanting our songs of Freedom, O.

Sailors took Hutchinson's words and Foster's tune, and created the sea chantey "Sacramento."

Sacramento

Words: Anonymous. Music: Stephen Foster.

CHORUS
Ho, boys, ho, for Californ-i-o!
There's plenty of gold so I've been told
On the banks of the Sacramento.

Eighteen hundred and forty-nine, duda, duda,
Eighteen hundred and forty-nine, ho duda day,
We set our stuns'ls on a quartering wind, duda, duda,
We set our stuns'ls on a quartering wind, ho duda day. CHORUS

We sailed away one day in May, duda, duda,
We sailed away one day in May, ho duda day.
Our sails were full on every stay, duda, duda,
Our sails were full on every stay, ho duda day. CHORUS

They're diggin' out gold with a spade and a pick, duda, duda,
They're diggin' out gold with a spade and a pick, ho duda day.
They're takin' out lumps as big as a brick, duda, duda,
They're takin' out lumps as big as a brick, ho duda day. CHORUS

The Big Five Gallon Jar

During the gold rush, sailors deserted their ships to head for the gold fields. Eventually more than four hundred ships were stranded in San Francisco's harbor for lack of crews, so shipowners arranged to kidnap crews. The men who shanghaied sailors were called "crimps." The crimps arranged with boarding house owners and barkeeps in the lawless Barbary Coast section to put dope in the drinks of unsuspecting customers. The next day the drugged victim would awaken on board a whaling ship headed for three years on the Bering Sea, or on a ship going around Cape Horn.

Eventually, the crimps and boarding house owners organized the Seaman's Landlord Protection Organization. They created an absolute monopoly, supplying sailors for nearly every ship in and out of San Francisco. They also controlled the rate of pay for the sailors, setting it high and keeping half of it for themselves, fleecing both the ship owners and the sailors. Shanghaiing was practiced openly in San Francisco for many years, making it the most notorious port in the world.

Sailors were shanghaied in other ports, too. "The Big Five Gallon Jar" has versions from Liverpool, Nova Scotia and New York. The names of the proprietors who plied the sailors with drugged beer or whiskey from their "big five gallon jars" vary, but the chorus is always *In the old Virginia lowlands, lowlands low*, suggesting that the song may have originated in the Chesapeake Bay. We learned this version from folksingers Dick Holdstock and Allan MacLeod.

The Glenesslin, Shipwrecked on the Oregon Coast

The Big Five Gallon Jar

Words and Music: Anonymous.

On the Bar-b'ry Coast there lived a man, his name was Lar-ry Marr, And in the days of the Cape Horn trade, he played the shang-hai game. His wife's name was Ma-ry Ann, they was known both near and far, They nev-er missed a luck-y chance to use the Big Five Gal-lon Jar. In the

Chorus old Vir-gin-ia Low-lands, Low-lands, low In the old Vir-gin-ia Low-lands, low.

On the Barbary Coast there lived a man, his name was Larry Marr,
And in the days of the Cape Horn trade, he played the shanghai game.
His wife's name was Mary Ann, they was known both near and far,
They never missed a lucky chance to use the Big Five Gallon Jar.

CHORUS
In the old Virginia lowlands, lowlands low,
In the old Virginia lowlands low.

Well a hell-ship she was short of men, of four red-blooded tars,
And Missus and Larry plied the beer in the Big Five Gallon Jar.
Shell-backs and farmers, just the same, sailed into Larry Marr's,
And sailed away on the skys'l ship, helped by the Big Five Gallon Jar. CHORUS

Well there was five or six old drunken tars all standin' around the bar,
And Larry he was serving them from the Big Five Gallon Jar.
Oh their names were known both near and far, as is the Cape Horn Bar,
And the dope they served to old Jack Tar from the Big Five Gallon Jar. CHORUS

From the Barbary Coast steer clear, my lads, and steer clear of Larry Marr,
Or else, damn sure shanghaied you'll be by the Big Five Gallon Jar,
Shanghaied away on a skys'l ship around Cape Horn so far,
Away from all the girls and boys, and the Big Five Gallon Jar! CHORUS

Like other western states, California produced its share of bandits. The most notorious was Joaquin Murieta, the most colorful, Black Bart. Black Bart robbed 28 stage coaches. He wore a flour sack over his head when he stopped a stage, and shouted "Throw down the box!" He also left a poem behind for his victims to read. The poem was signed with the letters PO followed by the number 8 (po-ate). One of his poems said:

So here I've stood while wind and rain
Have set the trees a-sobbin'
And risked my life for that damned stage
That wasn't worth the robbin'.

Black Bart was eventually caught, served five years at San Quentin Prison, and was never heard from again.

La Indita

California's Native American people paid a terrible price for the coming of the Europeans. By 1846, under Spanish and Mexican rule, the Indian population had decreased from 250,000 to 100,000. During the first twenty years under American domination, the population dropped to 30,000, and by the end of the 19th century, it was down to 16,000. European diseases caused about 60 percent of the deaths, and another 10 percent were killed by the newcomers.

California Indians sang "La Indita," about the coming of the white men. William J. McCoy collected a version from an old California mission Indian. Folklorist Charles Lummis collected a number of versions.

One version says *Ay Chihuahua cuantos Yanquis* (Yankees), another says *Ay Chihuahua cuanto huero* (light haired people).

The words mean: "When the Indians came down, the Indian maidens said, 'Ay Chihuahua, so many Yankees!' Ah, my friends, the poor Indians! But that's the way life goes."

La Indita

Words and Music: Anonymous.

Cuan-do los In-dios ba-ja-ran, Cuan-do los In-dios ba - ja - ran,

Y las In-di - tas di-cien-do, Ay chi-hua-hua, cuan-tos Yan-quis, Y las In - di -

tas di-cien-do, Ay chi-hua-hua, cuan-tos Yan-quis. Ay, ay,

ay ay ay, Ay, ay, ay ay ay. Ay co - ma - dre com -

pa - dre los In - dios, Ay co - ma - dre com - pa - dre los In - dios.

Si vay ve - ri, si vay ve - ri, Si vay ve - ri que may-ne ve. Si vay ve - ri,

si vay ve - ri, Si vay ve - ri que may - ne ve.

Cuando los Indios bajaran, cuando los Indios bajaran,
Y las Inditas diciendo, "Ay chihuahua cuantos Yanquis."
Y las Inditas diciendo, "Ay chihuahua cuantos Yanquis."
Ay, ay, ay, ay, ay. Ay, ay, ay, ay, ay,
Ay comadre, compadre los Indios. Ay comadre, compadre los Indios.
Si vay veri, si vay veri, si vay veri que mayne ve,
Si vay veri, si vay veri, si vay veri que mayne ve.

Mosa - Mohave

My Log Cabin Home

By 1860, two thirds of California's 380,000 non-Indian residents were American citizens. The other third included Chinese, Irish, Germans, English, Mexicans, Canadians, French, Scots, Italians and South Americans. Less than one out of four residents between the ages of 20 and 50 were women. The gold rush was coming to an end.

Stephen Foster's "My Old Kentucky Home" provided the melody for this song. "My Log Cabin Home" was published in *Put's Original California Songster* in 1855.

My Log Cabin Home

Words: John A. Stone. Music: Stephen Foster.

The tall pines wave, and the winds loudly roar,
No matter, keep digging away,
The wild flowers blossom 'round the log cabin door,
Where we sit after mining all the day.
A few more days and our mining all will end,
The canyon so rich will be dry,
The tools on the bank shall be left for a friend,
Then, my log cabin home, goodbye.

We'll hunt no more for the grizzly in the nook,
The Indians we'll soon leave behind,
We'll drink no more from the clear crystal brook,
As around the log cabin it winds.
The old oak tree, under which the cabin stands,
All shady at noon where we lie,
One final look at the old oak so grand,
Then, my log cabin home, goodbye.

Railroaders, Boom and Bust

I've Been Workin' on the Railroad

I've Been Workin' on the Railroad

Words and Music: Anonymous.

"I've Been Workin' on the Railroad" was published in *Carminia Princetonia*, a book of Princeton University students' songs, under the title "Levee Song," in 1894.

I've been work-in' on the rail - road, all the live - long day,

I've been work - in' on the rail - road, just to pass the time a - way,

Can't you hear the whis - tle blow - in', "Rise up so ear - ly in the morn."

Can't you hear the cap - tain shout - in', "Di - nah blow your horn."

I've been workin' on the railroad, all the live-long day.
I've been workin' on the railroad, just to pass the time away,
Can't you hear the whistle blowin' "Rise up so early in the morn!"
Can't you hear the captain shoutin' "Dinah, blow your horn!"

Building the Central Pacific

Subsidy

In 1859, civil engineer Theodore Judah helped persuade the California state legislature to consider building a railroad to the east across the Sierra Nevada mountains. He also convinced California businessmen Mark Hopkins, Collis Huntington, Leland Stanford and Charles Crocker, later known as the "Big Four," to organize the Central Pacific Railroad. Construction began in 1863. The Federal Government agreed to grant the railroads 6,400 acres of government land for each mile of track laid, and to loan $16,000 per mile of track laid on the plains, $32,000 per mile in the Great Basin, and $48,000 per mile in the mountains. In 1864, the Federal Government doubled the land grants.

Still not satisfied, Leland Stanford, president of the Central Pacific and governor of California, persuaded the state legislature to pay $10,000 for each mile of track laid in California. The railroad also received a half million dollars in loans from California's counties.

The words to "Subsidy" were published in the *California Mail Bag* in 1872. The tune is from the English music hall song "The Fine Old English Gentleman." During the 1840s American popular songwriter John Broughman borrowed the tune for his stage-Irish song "The Fine Old Irish Gentleman." Other songs using the same tune and format included the minstrel song "The Fine Old Colored Gentleman."

The reference in "Subsidy" about sending Sargent to the senate refers to California congressman Aaron Sargent. Sargent was the man who presented a geologist's report to President Lincoln indicating that soil washed down from the Sierra Nevada mountains was found seven miles east of Sacramento, the so-called "proof" that the mountains began 24 miles further west than they actually did. This gained nearly an additional million dollars for the Central Pacific. Sargent commented, "My pertinacity and Abraham's faith removed mountains."

Subsidy

Words and Music: Anonymous.

There is a corporation within this Golden State,
Which owns a line of railroads for conveying men and freight
To the Mormon town of Ogden at an elevated rate,
And which began in a very small way via the Dutch Flat swindle
      but by perseverance and bonds including subsidies
      became both strong and great,
For this Railroad Corporation is the deuce in subsidies.

Now this mighty Corporation had placed its terminus
At Sacramento City, after no small bit of fuss,
Whereat the San Franciscans raved and Oaklanders did cuss,
And tried their best to have a change, so that we of the Bay
      might have all the benefits, profits, and advantages
      come flowing unto us
Of this Railroad Corporation and its heap of subsidies.

First, San Francisco said 'twould give all down on Mission Bay,
If the Corporation would but make its terminus that way,
Some sixty acres more or less of finest kind of clay,
Which could be brought to the surface by a dredge with a ten-foot
      stroke or covered over with nice long piles if they wished
      to build a quay,
For this Railroad Corporation from its many subsidies.

The Railroad took the handsome gift, but said 'twould wait a while
Before it filled the marsh-land in or drove a single pile,
And then it went to Oakland, and with clever word and smile,
Agreed to make the terminus at that place if the city would donate
      all its waterfront and never expect the cars to stop within a mile,
For this Railroad Corporation is the deuce on subsidies.

Next the Corporation brought the old Vallejo route,
And then, before the people could mistrust what 'twas about,
It gobbled all the other roads, and then expressed a doubt
Concerning the permanent location of this remarkable terminus,
      which was as unreliable as a Spanish land title or an old
      black cat with a bad rheumatic gout,
For this Railroad Corporation wanted other subsidies.

And then this city rose from sleep, and in a hearty way,
Exclaimed, "If you'll come here we'll build a bridge across the Bay,
But the Corporation wrote a letter half a yard long, which,
      being interpreted, implied that the Corporation
      was on another lay,
For this Railroad Corporation has its eye on subsidies.

Then the people grew excited, and raised a hue and cry
Of "Anti-Subsidy," and vowed they never more would try
To help the Corporation, but would break its power by
A lot of incorruptible and undefiled Legislators, who had been
      elected for the express purpose of bestowing a black eye
On this Railroad Corporation which is fond of subsidies.

But when the Legislature met, the simple People found
That the Corporation's agents had been slyly prowling round,
Till the Legislators one and all had changed their stamping ground,
And voted as the railroad wished on every question, and sent
      Sargent to the Senate with the understanding that he
      should help Jim Nye and his *confreres* to expound
How this Railroad Corporation should have other subsidies.

And now that Stanford owns the railroads and the boats,
Half the State and more than half the Legislative votes,
For Frisco or for Oakland he doesn't care two goats,
And has decided to retire to a secluded isle of the sea sometimes
        called Yerba Buena, but more familiarly known as the
        Island of the Goats,
With his terminus, his railroad, and his lots of subsidies.

Which little rhyming narrative just shows us that, Whereas,
The Corporation's clever and the Public is an ass.
Resolved, the first must always win, the other go to grass,
Which happy consummation every one who has noted the brilliant efforts
        of a San Francisco community to make a commercial idiot of itself
        hopes soon may come to pass,
As also hopes the Railroad with its wealth of subsidies.

John Chinaman, My Jo

The Central Pacific needed thousands of men to build the railroad. When Charles Crocker hired a crew of Chinese workers, his construction boss, James Harvey Strobridge, objected. He thought the Chinese were too small, and not strong enough to do the heavy work required in building a railroad. Crocker replied, "They built the Great Wall of China, didn't they?" The Chinese were certainly strong enough, and were also less inclined to strike or to get drunk than Strobridge's predominantly Irish workers.

Crocker recruited first in California, and then in China, advancing each worker 25 to 40 dollars at five percent interest per month. White workers received free food and housing, while Chinese workers were required to pay for their food and provide their own housing. The Chinese were put into small crews of fifteen or twenty men, with a cook who could speak English to distribute wages and pay debts for the gang. Working three shifts per day, they soon dominated the Central Pacific's work force of ten thousand men. Ironically, none of the songs sung by the Chinese railroad workers have been preserved. The only songs to survive were the songs written and sung by whites about the Chinese.

Using the tune of Robert Burns's popular Scots song "John Anderson, My Jo," J. W. Conner published "John Chinaman, My Jo" in his *Conner's Irish Song Book* in 1868.

John Chinaman, My Jo

Words: J.W. Conner. Music: J.Watson.

John Chinaman, my jo, John, you're coming precious fast,
Each ship that sails from Shanghai brings an increase on the last,
And when you'll stop invading us, I'm blest, now, if I know,
You'll outnumber us poor Yankees, John Chinaman, my jo.

John Chinaman, my jo, John, you not only come in shoals,
But you often shake the washing stuff and spoil the water holes,
And, of course, that riles the miners, John, and enrages them, you know,
For they drive you frequently away, John Chinaman, my jo.

John Chinaman, my jo, John, you used to live on rice,
But now you purchase flour, plums, and other things that's nice,
And I see a butcher's shop, John, at your Chinese place below,
And you like your mutton now and then, John Chinaman, my jo.

John Chinaman, my jo, John, though folks at you may rail,
Here's blessings on your head, John, and more power to your tail,
But a bit of good advice, John, I'll give you ere I go,
Don't abuse the freedom you enjoy, John Chinaman, my jo.

Hayseed Like Me

On May 10, 1869, Leland Stanford of the Central Pacific and Thomas Durant of the Union Pacific drove the golden spike at Promontory, Utah, and the first transcontinental railroad began operation. Overnight, the time required to reach Sacramento from Omaha, Nebraska was reduced from four months to four days!

The Big Four then began to gobble up the smaller railroads in California, including the California & Central, the Yuba, and the San Francisco and San Jose Railroads. They also completed the Western Pacific from Sacramento to Oakland, and acquired franchises for the California & Oregon, and for the Southern Pacific. For a time, the Big Four controlled all transcontinental railroad traffic to and from California, and the Southern Pacific became known as "The Octopus."

In 1868 the Big Four acquired the charter and land grants to build a railroad from San Francisco to San Diego. The railroad was not ready to begin construction, so it postponed claiming title to its free government land grants. Since they could not yet sell the land, they distributed pamphlets inviting farmers to occupy and farm the future railroad property. The Big Four promised that they would sell the land to the farmers for about $2.50 per acre, with no charges for any improvements the farmers might make.

Farmers in the Mussell Slough district of the Central Valley took the railroad at its word, spending ten years constructing an elaborate irrigation system for their farm land. When the railroad finally took title to the land, instead of $2.50 per acre, they set prices ranging from $17 to $40 per acre. The angry farmers took their case to the U.S. Supreme Court. They lost the case, lost their improvements, and lost their farms.

These actions increased anti-railroad sentiment in California and other western states, and spurred western farmers to organize the People's Party of the United States of America, better known as the Populist Party.

This populist song was sung to the tune "Old Rosin the Beau," which came to America from Ireland in the early 19th century. It was used for many 19th century American songs including the campaign song "Lincoln and Liberty Too," the humorous song "Acres of Clams" and the shape note hymn "Sawyer's Exit."

The words to "Hayseed Like Me" were written by Arthur Kellogg, and published in the *Farmer's Alliance* in 1890.

THE STRUGGLE

OF THE

MUSSEL SLOUGH SETTLERS

FOR THEIR HOMES!

AN APPEAL TO THE PEOPLE

HISTORY OF THE LAND TROUBLES IN TULARE AND FRESNO COUNTIES.

THE GRASPING GREED OF THE RAILROAD MONOPOLY.

BY THE SETTLERS' COMMITTEE.

VISALIA:
Delta Printing Establishment,
1880.

Hayseed Like Me

Words: Arthur L. Kellogg. Music: Anonymous.

I once was a tool of oppression, as green as a sucker could be,
When monopolies banded together to beat a poor hayseed like me.

The railroads and old party bosses together did sweetly agree,
They thought there would be little trouble in workin' a hayseed like me.

CHORUS
In working' a hayseed like me, in workin' a hayseed like me,
They thought there would be little trouble in workin' a hayseed like me.

But now I've roused up a little, their greed and corruption I see,
And the ticket we vote next November will be made up of hayseeds like me.

CHORUS
Will be made up of hayseeds like me, will be made up of hayseeds like me,
And the ticket we vote next November, will be made up of hayseeds like me.

The Bummers' Hotel

The boom anticipated with the opening of the transcontinental railroad turned out to be a bust. Eastern firms imported goods by rail and undersold California manufacturers. The many thousands of Chinese railroad workers who had built the Central Pacific returned to California looking for work. Between 1870 and 1875, an additional eighty thousand Chinese migrated to California from China, expecting to find jobs. Thousands of immigrants from the eastern states poured into California to take part in the new boom. Instead, they all encountered an economic depression that lasted ten years. Unemployment estimates were as high as one hundred thousand. Low priced housing was in great demand.

I learned this song from my mother, Marion Oakley McNeil, who learned it from her father, William Calvin Oakley.

The Bummers' Hotel

Words and Music: Anonymous.

Oh my name is Mike Murphy, I come from Galore,
I had a large family so I opened a store.
I hired the whole house and the gang knew me well,
And the name that they gave it was the Bummers' Hotel.

CHORUS
Sure 'twas one cent for coffee, and two cents for bread,
Three for a beefsteak and five for a bed.
And the wind from the ocean gave a salt water smell
To the particular guests at the Bummers' Hotel.

Miss Judy O'Connor put her name on the book,
As head chamber maid and chief pastry cook,
She makes fine rat pies, too, like hotcakes they sell
To the particular guests at the Bummers' Hotel. CHORUS

I Had but Fifty Cents

In Southern California, from 1876 to 1880, Los Angeles' population dropped from 17,600 to 11,000 people. Many Californians found themselves unable to pay their bills.

Dan Lewis, who wrote "I Had but Fifty Cents," was a popular singer and entertainer during the 1870s and '80s.

This version also came from William Calvin Oakley, my grandfather.

I Had but Fifty Cents

Words and Music: Dan Lewis.

Well I took my gal to a fancy ball, it was a social hop,
We waited till the folks were gone and the music it did stop;
I took her to a restaurant, the best place on the street,
She said she wasn't hungry, but this is what she eat:
A dozen eggs raw, a plate of slaw, a chicken and a roast,
Some applesass, sparagrass, soft shelled crabs on toast,
A big box stew, and crackers, too, her appetite was immense!
When she asked for pie, I thought I'd die, 'cause I had but fifty cents.

She said she wasn't hungry, she didn't care to eat,
But I've got money in my coat to bet she can't be beat.
She took it in so cozy, she had an awful tank,
She said she wasn't thirsty, but this is what she drank:
A whiskey skin, a glass of gin, which filled my heart with fear,
A ginger pop with rum on top, a schooner then of beer,
A glass of ale, a gin cocktail, she shoulda had more sense,
When she asked for more I fell on the floor, 'cause I had but fifty cents.

Well of course I wasn't hungry, I didn't care to eat,
Expecting every moment to get kicked into the street,
She said she'd bring her family round, and we'd all have some fun,
When I gave the man my fifty cents, this is what he done:
He tore my clothes, he smashed my nose, he hit me in the jaw,
He gave me a prize of a pair of black eyes, and with me swept the floor.
He grabbed me where my pants hung loose and threw me over the fence,
Now take my advice, and don't try it twice, if you have but fifty cents!

Economic recovery began when the Southern Pacific Railroad pushed across the Southwest, and opened up the "Sunset Route" from California to New Orleans. This, plus extensive advertising and promotion, helped create a population explosion, a real estate boom, new towns, and new farms in Southern California. The boom was enhanced in 1885 when the Atchison, Topeka and Santa Fe Railroad completed their line from Kansas City to San Diego and Los Angeles.

As the 19th century drew to a close, Californians anticipated the new century with excitement and high expectations.

Farmers and Ranchers

California Here I Come

M. Witmark & Sons published this California favorite in 1924.

California Here I Come

Words and Music: Al Jolson, Bud De Silva and Joseph Meyer.

right back where I start - ed from,

Where bow - ers of flow - ers bloom in the spring,

Each morn - ing, at dawn - ing, bird - ies sing and ev - 'ry thing. A

sun - kist miss said, "Don't be late."

That's why I can hard - ly wait,

O - pen up that Gold - en Gate, Cal - i -

for - nia, here I come.

When the wintry winds are blowing, and the snow is starting in to fall,
Then my eyes turn westward, knowing that's the place I love the best of all.
California, I've been blue, since I've been away from you,
I can't wait till I get going, even now I'm starting in to call Oh,

CHORUS
California, here I come, right back where I started from,
Where bowers of flowers bloom in the spring,
Each morning, at dawning, birdies sing and everything,
A sun-kist miss said, "Don't be late." That's why I can hardly wait,
Open up that Golden Gate, California, here I come.

Any one who likes to wander, ought to keep this saying in his mind,
"Absence makes the heart grow fonder," of the good old place you left behind.
When you've hit the trail a while, seems you rarely see a smile;
That's why I must fly out yonder, where a frown is mighty hard to find! Oh, CHORUS

California Oranges

Beginning with the reclamation of the Central Valley by Chinese farm workers, California's agriculture evolved into the most varied and profitable in the Western Hemisphere. California provided soil and climatic conditions unparalleled anywhere for high production farming.

In the 1860s, state commissioner Agoston Haraszthy imported 1,400 varieties of grape cuttings from Europe, laying the foundation for California's celebrated wine industry.

In the early 1870s, Eliza Tibbets imported two navel orange trees from Bahia, Brazil to Riverside. In less than 10 years, Riverside gained national recognition for its delicious navel oranges. By 1900 there were more than five and a half million orange trees in Southern California. Children in Riverside jumped rope to this chant:

California Oranges

Words: Anonymous.

California oranges, tap me on the back, the back, the back, the back,
California oranges, tap me on the back, the back, the back, the back.
California oranges, tap me on the back, the back, the back, the back.
How many oranges can you eat?
One, two, three, four, five, six, seven, eight, nine, ten, eleven...
(until the jump is missed)

Andre Madalen

California's livestock industry began with the establishment of the missions. The sheep industry expanded with the demand for meat and wool during the gold rush, and the demand for wool during the Civil War. Between 1850 and 1870, California's sheep population increased from about 17 thousand to nearly three million.

Sheep herders during and after the gold rush were mostly Chinese, Portuguese, French and Basque.

The Basque presence dated back well before the gold rush, as some of California's governors under Spanish rule were Basque. However, the man who became known as the Father of American Basques arrived in 1849. His name was Pedro Altube, and he had herded sheep on the *pampas* in South America before coming to California. Word reached the French and Spanish Pyrenees that in California a man herding sheep could be paid in ewes to start his own herd, and he could graze sheep free on government land. For generations, young Basque

men migrated to California to become sheep-herders. Basque communities in Chino, Bakersfield, Fresno and San Francisco continue to sing and dance to the music of their Basque ancestors.

"Andre Madalen" is often sung at a Basque *trikitixa* (fandango) in California, and the people dance to the song. The lyrics in this song, and in many of the songs sung at a *trikitixa* are nonsensical. The lyrics say: "One day I was looking for my wife and I was told, 'she is drunk, don't pay her any mind.' Andre Madalen, Andre Madalen, half a quart of oil. The wife gets in debt and later the husband will pay. My wife knows how to sew and iron, but the thing she prefers over all is the white wine in her soup."

Andre Madalen

Words and Music: Anonymous.

En - e an-dre-ak ba-da-ki jos-ten, e - ta li-sat-zen tau-la

gai - ne - an, Ar - no xu - ri - a sal-dan e - man-ik, mai-te du or-oz

gai - ne - tik. *Chorus* An-dre Ma-da-len, An-dre Ma-da-len laur-den

er - di bat ol - i - o! Ai-tak sa - ri - a e-kar-

rit - zi - an, a - mak or-dain-du-ko di - o.

Ene andreak badaki josten,
eta lisatzen taula gainean;
Arno xuria saldan emanik,
maite du oroz gainetik.

CHORUS
Andre Madalen, Andre Madalen,
laurden erdi bat olio!
Aitak saria ekarritzian,
amak ordainduko dio.

Egun batean ni ari nintzen,
andrea ezin ikusirik.
Erran zautetan: "edana dago,
ez egin hari kasurik!"

Bere gizona utzik etxean,
hantxe da bera patar batean:
Indarrik gabe, mozkorrarekin,
lurrerat joaiten da behin!

El Rancho Grande

Many of the huge cattle ranches in Northern California disappeared during the gold rush. However the Southern California ranches remained intact and prospered through the 1850s as gold seekers increased their demand for beef. The cattle drives from Southern to Northern California were similar in many ways to the later cattle drives from Texas to Kansas. Severe thunderstorms, Indian raids, stampedes and cattle rustlers plagued the *vaqueros*, as tens of thousands of cattle were driven north to feed the miners.

This traditional 19th century song was popular in California and the Texas/Mexican border area.

The words mean:

Over at the big ranch where I used to live was a young lady who said to me, "I will make you some pants like the ranch owner wears. I'll begin making them with wool and finish them with leather. Don't ever trust promises, especially promises of love, because if they give you pumpkins [reject you] you'll feel great embarrassment. Pay close attention when the door squeaks. The dead don't make any noise [old proverb meaning no matter how hard you listen you can't hear] and their grief is heavy.

When someone asks for a cigar, don't give him a cigar and matches. If you give him both things, he'll take you to be a skunk."

Roping and Branding

El Rancho Grande

Words and Music: Anonymous.

CHORUS
Allá en el rancho grande,
Allá donde vivía,
Había una rancherita,
Que alegre me decía,
Que alegre me decía:

Te voy a hacer tus calzones,
Como los usa el ranchero,
Te los comienzo de lana,
Te los acabo de cuero.

Nunca te fíes de promesas
Ni mucho menos de amores,
Que si te dan calabazas,
Verás lo que son ardores.

Pon muy atento el oído,
Cuando rechine la puerta,
Hay muertos que no hacen ruído
Y son muy gordas sus penas.

Cuando te pidan cigarro,
No des cigarro y cerillo,
Porque si das las dos cosas
Te tantearán de zorrillo.

Come Day Go Day, Wish It Was Sunday
Rye Whiskey • Cindy

The drought of 1860 reduced the cattle population from 70,000 to 20,000. Despite this setback, cattle raising remained an important California industry. The ranchers and cowboys sang the songs they learned from the *vaqueros*, songs that they wrote themselves and songs they brought with them from other states.

My great-grandfather, Cary Calvin Oakley, brought these songs to California when he crossed the plains from Lebanon, Tennessee in 1850. He taught them to his son William Calvin Oakley, who raised cattle on the Alamo Ranch, near Santa Maria, California.

Come Day Go Day, Wish It Was Sunday

Words and Music: Anonymous.

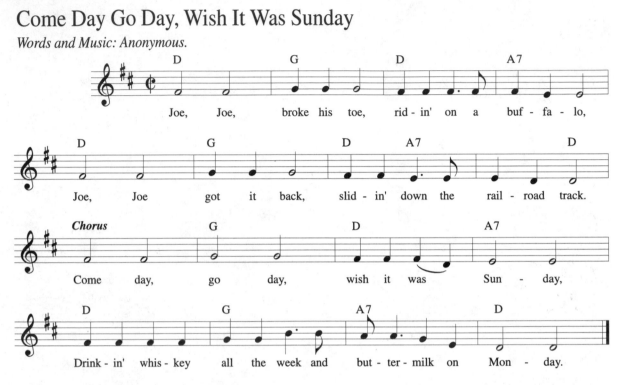

Joe, Joe, broke his toe, rid-in' on a buf-fa-lo,

Joe, Joe got it back, slid-in' down the rail-road track.

Chorus
Come day, go day, wish it was Sun-day,

Drink-in' whis-key all the week and but-ter-milk on Mon-day.

Joe, Joe broke his toe, ridin' on a buffalo,
Joe, Joe got it back, slidin' down the railroad track.

CHORUS
Come day, go day, wish it was Sunday,
Drinkin' whiskey all the week and buttermilk on Monday.

Squire's dog came to town, by the name of Towser,
Squire Jack sent him back, and said you'd better scram, sir.
CHORUS

Joe cut off his big toe and hung it up to dry,
All the girls began to laugh, and Joe began to cry. CHORUS

Rye Whiskey

Words and Music: Anonymous.

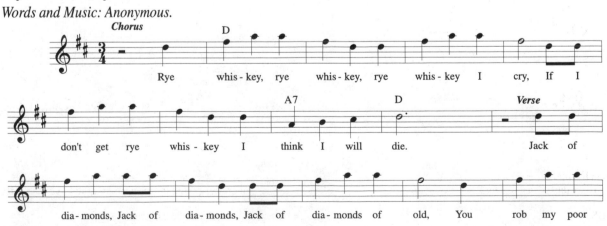

Rye whis-key, rye whis-key, rye whis-key I cry, If I

don't get rye whis-key I think I will die. Jack of

dia-monds, Jack of dia-monds, Jack of dia-monds of old, You rob my poor

         pock - ets   of   sil - ver   and   gold.

CHORUS
Rye whiskey, rye whiskey, rye whiskey I cry,
If I don't get rye whiskey I think I will die.

Jack of diamonds, Jack of diamonds, Jack of diamonds of old,
You rob my poor pockets of silver and gold. CHORUS

I'll eat when I'm hungry, I'll drink when I'm dry,
And if whiskey don't kill me, I'll live till I die. CHORUS

Oh Lulu, oh Lulu, oh Lulu my dear,
I'd give the whole world if my Lulu was here. CHORUS

If the ocean was whiskey and I was a duck,
I'd dive to the bottom and never come up. CHORUS

Cindy

Words and Music: Anonymous.

I get up in the mornin' go out upon my farm, Lucinda is my darlin' and she took me by the arm. She took me to her parlor, she cooled me with her fan, She swore I was the prettiest thing in the shape of mortal man. Get along home, little Lucindy, get along home, little Lucindy, Get along home, little Lucindy, get along home to mammy-o.

I get up in the mornin' go out upon my farm,
Lucinda is my darlin' and she took me by the arm.

CHORUS
Get along home little Lucindy, get along home little Lucindy,
Get along home little Lucindy, get along home to mammy-o.

She took me to her parlor, she cooled me with her fan,
She swore I was the prettiest thing in the shape of mortal man. CHORUS

She told me that she loved me, she called me "Sugar Plum,"
She throwed her arms around me, Lord, I thought my time had come. CHORUS

The Strawberry Roan

America's favorite cowboy ballad is "The Strawberry Roan." The words were written by Curley Fletcher, a Californian who punched cattle in the Owens Valley early in the 20th century. *The Boulder Creek News* published Fletcher's poem "The Outlaw Broncho" [sic] in 1914. By 1917 Fletcher had changed the name of his poem to "The Strawberry Roan" and published it, along with some of his other poems, in a book titled *Rhymes of the Roundup*. Someone added the tune, and Fletcher's "Strawberry Roan" spread quickly throughout the cowboy community.

Unfortunately, Fletcher received very little compensation for writing what has become the most popular of all the bucking horse songs.

The term "the blinds" refers to a leather blindfold used when saddling an unruly horse. When the horse twists his body alternately to the right and left, in the shape of a crescent, he is "sunfishing." "Caballo" means horse in Spanish. If a cowboy is "grabbing the apple" or "pulling leather," he is holding onto the saddle horn. When the horse stiffens his legs and arches his back he is "frog-walking" or "crow hopping."

I learned the song from my great-uncle Lewis Oakley, a California cowboy.

The Strawberry Roan

Words: Curley Fletcher. Music: Anonymous.

I was loafin' around, just spendin' my time, out of a job, hadn't a dime,
A feller steps up and he says, "I suppose that you're a bronc fighter, by the looks of your clothes."
Well I thought he was right and I told him the same, and I asks has he got any bad ones to tame,
He says he's got one, and a good one to buck, fer pilin' good cowboys he's had lots of luck.

Well I gets all excited, and I asks what he pays to ride that old pony for a couple of days,
He offers ten dollars, says I, "I'm your man, 'cause the bronc never lived that I couldn't fan.
Well I don't like to brag, but I got this to say, that I ain't been throwed for many a day."
He says, "Get your saddle, I'll give you a chance." So we gets in his buckboard and we drifts to his ranch.

I stays until mornin' and right after chuck, I steps out to see if that outlaw can buck.
He was down in the hoss corral standin' alone, a snaky-eyed outlaw, a strawberry roan,
His legs was all spavined, he's got pigeon toes, little pig eyes and a long Roman nose,
Little pin ears that touched at the tip with an XYZ iron stamped on his left hip.

He's ewe-necked and old with a long lower jaw, all the things that you'll see on a wild outlaw.
Well I puts on my spurs, I'm sure feelin' fine, turns up my hat and I picks up my twine.
I piled my loop on him, and well I knew then, that before he's rode I'd sure earn that ten,
I gets the blinds on him, it sure is a fight, next comes my saddle and I screws her down tight.

When I gets on him, I says, "Raise the blind, move out of his way, let's see him unwind."
He bows his old neck and I guess he unwound, he ain't spendin' much of his time on the ground,
He turns his old belly right up to the sun, he sure is a sun-fishin' son of a gun,
He goes up towards the east, comes down towards the west, to stay in his middle I'm a-doin' my best.

Well he's the worst bucker I've seen on the range, he could turn on a nickel and give you back change.
He hits on all fours and he turns on his side and I don't see how he keeps from losin' his hide,
I'll tell you no foolin' that caballo can step, but I'm still in my saddle and I'm buildin' some rep.
Away goes my stirrups, I loses my hat, I'm grabbin' the apple, and blind as a bat.

He sure is frog-walkin' he heaves a big sigh, he only lacks wings for to be on the fly,
And while he's a buckin', he squeals like a shoat, I tell you that pony has sure got my goat.
With a phenomenal jump he kicks her in high, and I'm sittin' on nothin' way up in the sky.
I turns over twice and I comes back to earth, and I lights in to cussin' the day of his birth.

Well I know that there's hosses I'm unable to ride, some is still livin' they haven't all died,
And I'll bet all my money that no man alive can stay on old Strawberry when he makes his high dive.

Breaking Horses

Temperance and Suffrage, Cars and Movie Stars

I'm On the Water Wagon Now

In the late 19th century, heavy drinking was still a major part of the California life style, and comic songs about drinking were popular. Being "on the water wagon" meant you were no longer drinking alcoholic beverages.

The song was published in 1903 by M. Witmark & Sons. I learned this version from my mother, Marion Oakley McNeil.

I'm On the Water Wagon Now

Words and Music: Paul West and John W. Bratton.

One night I came home late, pretty well lit up, looked around for one more drink, found something in a cup, I drank it very quickly, then tumbled into bed, Next morn' my wife awakened me, "Get up, we're robbed," she said, "I left two point laced tidies in a cup to soak," said she, "Can't find them any place, where on earth could they be?" I acted very innocent, but had to own my sin, For Irish point lace whiskers were a-sprouting on my chin, I'm on the water wagon now, I never get a jag on now. I'm improving in my habits no more snakes nor purple rabbits, 'Cause I'm on the water wagon now.

One night I came home late, pretty well lit up,
Looked around for one more drink, found something in a cup,
I drank it very quickly, then tumbled into bed,
Next morn' my wife awakened me, "Get up, we're robbed!" she said,
"I left two point lace tidies in a cup to soak," said she,
"Can't find them any place, where on earth could they be?"
I acted very innocent, but had to own my sin,
For Irish point lace whiskers were a-sprouting on my chin.

CHORUS
I'm on the water wagon now, I never get a jag on now.
I'm improving in my habits, no more snakes nor purple rabbits,
'Cause I'm on the water wagon now.

One night I met a college chum I hadn't seen for years,
We razzle dazzled round the town, gave the college cheers,
Just about the break of day, we thought for home we'd start,
When to our great dismay we couldn't tell ourselves apart.
We went to his address, or mine, we didn't know,
Sat down and waited for our wife to show,
And when at last she did appear, we cried in accents dim,
"Your husband's here come down and see which one of us is him!"

CHORUS
I'm on the water wagon now, I never get a jag on now.
Yes, I spend my nights in slumber, know my name, address and number,
'Cause I'm on the water wagon now.

The fateful day that I swore off I never shall forget,
The papers printed extras, 'twas exciting, you can bet,
Bartenders begged me not to quit, they cried with bated breath
That if I did their families would surely starve to death.
Cab drivers wept to think that they would drive me home no more,
Distilleries and breweries have "to let" upon the door,
And eighty-two drink chemists who had places on my beat,
Have had to quit their business and are working in the street.

CHORUS
For I'm on the water wagon now, I never get a jag on now.
Keely Cures and Carrie Nation point to me with admiration,
'Cause I'm on the water wagon now.

The Whiskey Shops Must Go

For many women, a heavy drinking husband was not a laughing matter. At the beginning of the 20th century, California women were actively pushing the causes of temperance and woman suffrage. Speakers at temperance meetings in California began espousing these "radical" ideas, and songs were powerful tools for creating enthusiasm for the causes. The Women's Christian Temperance Union was gaining strength, and temperance songs were resounding through the halls at WCTU rallies.

Sung to the tune of "The Battle Hymn Of The Republic," "The Whiskey Shops Must Go" appeared in a number of temperance song books published in the early twentieth century.

Songs of Might
To Cheer the Fight Against the Blight Of Liquordom

By CHARLES M. and J. H. FILLMORE

PRICES: Single copy, 25 cents; per dozen, by express, not prepaid, $2.40; per 100, by express, not prepaid, $20.00

Fillmore Music House

528 ELM STREET   CINCINNATI, O.

The Whiskey Shops Must Go

Words: W.W. Pinson. Music: Anonymous.

Oh, comrades in this conflict of the right against the wrong,
To the battle of the ballots come with shouting and with song,
And this shall be our slogan as the legions march along:
"The whiskey shops must go."

Jehovah's wrath is kindled, and His arm is lifted high,
For from out the dust of ages He has heard the martyrs cry,
The cup of wrath is brimming, and His vengeance draweth nigh,
"The whiskey shops must go."

CHORUS
Rally! rally! O ye free men! Rally! rally! O ye free men!
Rally! rally! O ye free men! The whiskey shops must go!

From the silence and the shadows, where our mothers weep and pray,
With their patient hands uplifted 'gainst the woe they cannot stay,
We have heard a voice entreating us to sweep the curse away,
"The whiskey shops must go."

Hear the children cry for pity from the cruel heart of greed,
See them trampled into silence by the monster while they plead!
Be quick, my patriot brothers, to the rescue let us speed,
"The whiskey shops must go." CHORUS

We are coming, we are coming! for the light has dawned at last,
Hark, the battle cry is ringing, and our lines are length'ning fast,
For God, and Home, and Native Land, our ballots shall be cast,
"The whiskey shops must go." CHORUS

Some Little Bug Is Going to Find You Some Day

By the beginning of the 20th century, Americans were aware that microorganisms cause disease, and many Californians became obsessed with germs.

"Some Little Bug," published in 1915, was written for the musical *Alone at Last* which played at the Schubert Theater on Broadway, and "celebrated the influenza epidemic of that year." Although the music is credited to Silvid Hein, it bears a striking similarity to "John Brown's Body."

I learned this version from my mother, and my aunt Elizabeth Oakley May.

Some Little Bug Is Going to Find You Someday

Words: Benjamin Hapgood Burt and Roy Atwell. Music: Silvid Hein.

In these days of indigestion there is often times a question
As to what to eat and what to leave alone.
For each microbe and bacillus has a special way to kill us,
And in time he always claims us for his own.

CHORUS
Some little bug is going to find you some day,
Some little bug will creep behind you some day,
Then he'll call in his bug friends and all your earthly trouble ends,
Yes, some little bug will find you some day.

Eating juicy sliced pineapple makes the sexton dust the chapel,
You only need one bite and that's enough.
Eat a plate of fine pig's knuckles and the undertaker chuckles
While your relatives start scrappin' 'bout your stuff.

CHORUS
Some little bug is going to find you some day,
Some little bug will creep behind you some day,
Then he'll settle on your gizzard, if you lose him you're a wizard,
Yes, some little bug will find you some day.

Eating lobster cooked or plain is only flirting with ptomaine,
While an oyster sometimes has a lot to say.
But the clams we eat in chowder make the angels chant the louder,
For they know that we'll be with them right away.

CHORUS
Some little bug is going to find you some day,
Some little bug will creep behind you some day,
He'll invade your green cucumber, he is sure to get your number,
Yes, some little bug will find you some day.

Eating huckleberry pie is a pleasing way to die,
While sauerkraut brings on softening of the brain.
When you eat banana fritters every undertaker titters,
And the casket makers nearly go insane.

CHORUS
Some little bug is going to find you some day,
Some little bug will creep behind you some day,
Then with a nervous little quiver
He'll give you cirrhosis of the liver,
Yes, some little bug will find you one day.

Lydia Pinkham

Manufacturers of patent medicines were quick to capitalize on the germ scare. Some patent medicine companies published song books, filled with testimonials for their products, which claimed to cure nearly every disease known to man. *The Red Z Songbook* dated 1906, distributed by California drug stores, advertised Simmons Liver Regulator. Some of the ailments which this product claimed to cure were: "*...Fever, ague, dropsy, jaundice, restlessness, heartburn, sick headache, languor, sour stomach, nausea, giddiness, foul breath, depression of spirits, malaria, marsh fever, coated tongue, lost appetite, yellow complexion, chills, pains in the back, dyspepsia, biliousness, dizziness and dimming of vision. It regulates the liver, protects the system from miasmatic influences, purifies and enriches the blood, assists digestion and builds up the system. And, as a remedy for diseases common among horses, cows, sheep, dogs and chickens, Simmons Regulator is without an equal. It should always be kept on hand in case of an attack of colic, worms or grubs, lack of condition, mange or chicken cholera.*"

Kickapoo Oil also sold well in California. The Kickapoo Indian Medicine Company advertised that each fluid ounce was 56.4 percent alcohol, contained eleven twentieths of a grain of opium, and eight minims of ether.

However, the most popular patent medicine in the early 20th century was Lydia Pinkham's Vegetable Compound. Lydia Pinkham turned her home remedy into a business in Lynn, Massachusetts, in 1873. The ingredients in Lydia Pinkham's Vegetable Compound included licorice, camomile, aletrus, pleurisy root, Jamaica dogwood, black cohosh, life plant, dandelion root and alcohol. After a few years, she reduced the alcohol content from 18 percent to 12 or 13 percent.

Lydia Pinkham

Words: Anonymous. Music: James McGranahan.

Now we'll sing of Ly-di-a - Pink-ham and her love for the hu - man race, How she sold her vege-ta - ble com-pound and the pa - pers pub-lished her face. It sells for a dol-lar a bot-tle which is ver-y cheap you see, And if it does-n't cure you, - she will sell you six for three.

Now we'll sing of Lydia Pinkham and her love for the human race,
How she sold her Vegetable Compound, and the papers published her face.
It sells for a dollar a bottle, which is very cheap, you see,
And if it doesn't cure you, she will sell you six for three.

Mrs. Smith, she had no children, it was hard for her to bear,
So she took some Vegetable Compound, now the Smiths are everywhere.

It sells for a dollar a bottle, which is very cheap, you see,
And if it doesn't cure you, she will sell you six for three.

Lydia Pinkham's slogan was, "There's a baby in every bottle." Another of the many verses to the song said:

*"There's a baby in every bottle." So the advertisements ran,
But the Federal Trade Commission still insists you'll need a man!*

Where Is My Wanderin' Ma Tonight?

Songs helped raise the spirits of groups working in California to achieve woman suffrage. Satire was often employed in the suffrage songs — and with good reason. For what could be more ironic than to have drunkards and fools allowed to vote just because they were men, while scholars, crusaders and leading citizens should be denied the vote just because they were women?

However, not all songs dealing with woman suffrage were favorable to the cause. The bloomer girls and their parades, the many dramatic devices employed by the women to call attention to women's rights, and the idea of suffragettes in general became subjects for abuse and ridicule.

"Where Is My Wanderin' Ma Tonight?" is a parody of Robert Lowry's "Where Is My Boy Tonight?." My mother and her sisters sang it to tease their mother, Bertha Belle Oakley, an active supporter of California's woman suffrage movement.

Where Is My Wanderin' Ma Tonight?
Words: Anonymous. Music: Robert Lowry.

Where is my wanderin' ma tonight, my mother oh where is she?
She's hied her off to the suffrage fight, and she didn't come home to tea.

CHORUS
The fire is cold in the kitchen range, the cupboard is bleak and bare,
And mother has gone to the county jail, for pulling the speaker's hair.

Where is my wanderin' ma tonight, my mother oh where is she?
She dwells in the box, while father's socks are holey as they can be. CHORUS

In 1911 California became the sixth state in the union to grant full suffrage to women.

He'd Have to Get Under - Get Out and Get Under

The automobile began to compete with the horse-drawn carriage early in the 20th century. California's roadways, however, had been designed for horses, not motor cars.

Added to the inadequate roads were the mechanical troubles that characterized these new-fangled machines. Al Jolson's hit song of 1913 became very popular in California.

He'd Have to Get Under - Get Out and Get Under

Words: Grant Clarke and Edgar Leslie. Music: Maurice Abrahams.

John-ny O' Con - nor bought an au-to-mo-bile, he took his sweet-heart for a ride one Sun - day, John-ny was togged up in his best Sun-day clothes, she nest-led close to his side. Things went just dan - dy 'till he got down the road, then some-thing hap - pened to the old ma - chine-ry, That en-gine got his goat, off went his hat and coat, ev - 'ry-thing need - ed re-pairs.

Chorus He'd have to get un - der, get out and get un-der, to fix his lit - tle ma - chine, He was just - dy - ing to cud-dle his queen, but ev' - ry

min - ute   when he'd be - gin it, He'd   have to get un - der, get

out and get un - der,   then he'd get   back   at the   wheel,

A - doz - en   times they'd   start   to   hug and kiss,   and then that

darned old   en - gine   it would miss,   And then he'd   have to get un -

der,   get   out   and   get un - - - der,   and

fix   up his au - - to - mo - bile.

Johnny O'Connor bought an automobile,
he took his sweetheart for a ride one Sunday,
Johnny was togged up in his best Sunday clothes,
she nestled close to his side.
Things went just dandy till he got down the road,
then something happened to the old machinery,
That engine got his goat, off went his hat and coat,
everything needed repairs.

CHORUS
He'd have to get under, get out and get under,
to fix his little machine,
He was just dying to cuddle his queen,
but every minute, when he'd begin it,
He'd have to get under get out and get under,
then he'd get back at the wheel,
A dozen times they'd start to hug and kiss,
and then that darned old engine it would miss,
And then he'd have to get under, get out and get under,
and fix up his automobile.

Millionaire Wilson said to Johnny one day,
"Your little sweetheart don't appreciate you,
I have a daughter who is hungry for love,
she likes to ride, by the way."
Johnny had visions of a million in gold,
he took her riding in his little auto,
But every time that he went to say "marry me,"
'twas the old story again. CHORUS

AL JOLSON'S TERRIFIC HIT!
HE'D HAVE TO GET UNDER-
GET OUT AND GET UNDER
(TO FIX UP HIS AUTOMOBILE)

WORDS BY
GRANT CLARKE &
EDGAR LESLIE
MUSIC BY
MAURICE ABRAHAMS

MAURICE ABRAHAMS MUSIC CO.
1570 BROADWAY
NEW YORK

AL JOLSON

The Jitney Bus

As the sale of automobiles increased, many people hired their cars out at a nickel a ride. These entrepreneurs referred to their horseless carriages as "jitney buses."

I learned this song from my mother, who learned it in 1916 while attending the California State Normal School in San Francisco.

The Jitney Bus

Words and Music: Anonymous.

Fa-ther is driv-ing a jit-ney bus from the sta-tion to the park, And soon I know he'll be a mil-lion-aire, The range in the kitch-en has been ig-nored, Dear moth-er is driv-ing a "can't af-ford," For half a dime she'll take you an-y-where, Sis-ter has left the de-part-ment store to be-come a jit-ney queen, Her lit-tle car is gain-ing great re-nown, The bank ac-count is get-ting fat, For Ma and Pa and sis-ter Hat, Since the jit-ney bus has come to bless our town.

Father is driving a jitney bus from the station to the park,
And soon I know he'll be a millionaire,
The range in the kitchen has been ignored,
Dear mother is driving a "can't afford,"
For half a dime she'll take you anywhere.
Sister has left the department store to become a jitney queen,
Her little car is gaining great renown,
The bank account is getting fat,
For ma and pa and sister Hat,
Since the jitney bus has come to bless our town.

In My Merry Oldsmobile

The state's love affair with automobiles continued to grow, and by 1925 the city of Los Angeles boasted one automobile for every three people — more than twice the national average!

Two Oldsmobiles crossed the United States from Detroit to Oregon in 1905, inspiring this song, which was published that same year.

In My Merry Oldsmobile

Words : Vincent Bryan. Music: Gus Edwards.

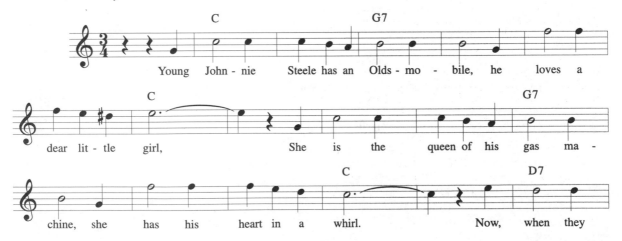

Young John-nie Steele has an Olds-mo-bile, he loves a dear lit-tle girl, She is the queen of his gas ma-chine, she has his heart in a whirl. Now, when they

Young Johnnie Steele has an Oldsmobile, he loves a dear little girl,
She is the queen of his gas machine, she has his heart in a whirl.
Now, when they go for a spin you know, she tries to learn the auto, so
He lets her steer while he gets her ear, and whispers soft and low:

CHORUS
Come away with me Lucile, in my merry Oldsmobile,
Down the road of life we'll fly automobubbling, you and I,
To the church we'll swiftly steal, and our wedding bells will peal,
You can go as far as you like with me in my Merry Oldsmobile.

They love to spark in the dark old park, as they go flying along,
She says she knows why the motor goes, the sparker's awfully strong.
Each day they spoon to the engine's tune, their honeymoon will happen soon,
He'll win Lucile with his Oldsmobile and then he'll fondly croon: CHORUS

Silent Movie Music

The invention of the movie camera rivaled the internal combustion engine as a development of major social impact during the first half of the 20th century. In 1899, William Dickson, working in the Edison laboratory in West Orange, New Jersey, created the first effective method of producing moving pictures on strips of celluloid. Most of the early motion pictures were produced in New York and New Jersey. Patents for projectors and cameras belonged to Edison and a few others, but outlaw film producers ignored the patents and began making films in Southern California. The distance between California and New York, as well the close proximity to the Mexican border, helped California's outlaw film-makers avoid the process servers. By 1910, helped along by the popularity of westerns, the center of the film industry was shifting from New York to Hollywood.

Before 1927, motion pictures were silent, and theaters used live music to create appropriate moods. Very large theaters often employed a full orchestra. However, most movie theaters used a piano or an organ. The piano player or the organist worked from cue sheets containing music designed for specific scenes. These cue sheets proved invaluable for the piano players and organists in silent movie theaters. The compositions here were written and played before the 1920s. The piano scores are courtesy of the Motion Picture Academy of Arts and Sciences, Center for Motion Picture Study, Margaret Herrick Library.

Silent Movie Camera

A joyful crowd, a pursuit, or a race.

Allegro Number One

Composed by Adolf Minot in 1915

A cattle stampede.

Western Allegro

Composed by Edward Falck in 1918

Piano

An Indian war dance.

Indian War Dance

Composed by Gaston Borch in 1918

Silent Movie - "The Story of Daniel Boone"

Fear, anxiety, suspense, ominous situations.

Agitato Misterioso

Composed by Otto Langey in 1918

The chase.

Hurry

Composed by Harry Norton in 1918

In 1924 G. Schirmer published *Motion Picture Moods for Pianists and Organists: A Rapid Reference Collection of Selected Pieces, Adapted to 52 Moods and Situations*, arranged by Erno Rapée. Rapée's book became the standard for the "silents."

San Francisco

The first major film with a soundtrack was *The Jazz Singer* starring Al Jolson. The "talkies" as they were called, swept the nation. Actors and actresses with poor voices disappeared from the silver screen. The industry flourished in Hollywood, and by the 1930s, was producing such classics as *Gone With the Wind* and *San Francisco*. The film *San Francisco*, starring Clark Gable, Jeannette MacDonald and Spencer Tracy, featured dramatic special effects depicting the disastrous earthquake and fire that destroyed the city in 1906. The film also featured the song "San Francisco," which was published in 1936.

San Francisco

Lyrics: Gus Kahn. Music: Bronislaw Kaper and Walter Jurmann.

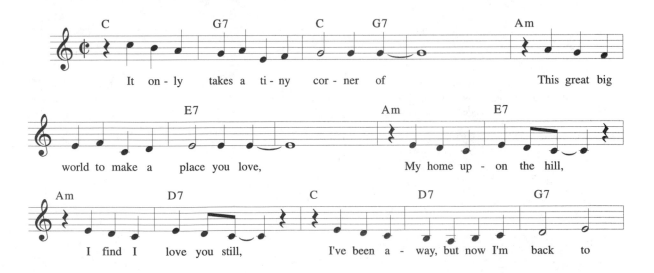

It on-ly takes a ti-ny cor-ner of This great big world to make a place you love, My home up-on the hill, I find I love you still, I've been a-way, but now I'm back to

It only takes a tiny corner of
This great big world to make a place you love,
My home upon the hill, I find I love you still,
I've been away, but now I'm back to tell you:

CHORUS
San Francisco, open your golden gate,
You let no stranger wait outside your door,
San Francisco here is your wandering one
Saying, "I'll wander no more."
Other places only make me love you best,
Tell me you're the heart of all the golden west,
San Francisco welcome me home again,
I'm coming home to go roaming no more.

Immigrants and Dust Bowl Refugees

We're Coming Back to California

The World War I song "We're Coming Back To California" became the "U.S. Government Official Song of the 40th (Sunshine) Division" on April 1, 1918. It was approved by command of Major General Strong, Major of Infantry, Division Adjutant. The Sunshine Division was headquartered at Camp Kearney, California.

We're Coming Back to California

Words: Ralph Hogan. Music: Frank Walterstein.

Hon - ey girl don't sigh, dry those tears don't cry, I'll be com - ing back some day; Though you write, you're blue, lit - tle girl so true, be-cause you know I'm far a - way. You know I love you best, girl of the Gold - en West, and the land of the West - ern Sun. I'll pack up right a-way for the old U. S. A. for when this war is won, I'm com - ing back to Cal - i - for - nia, to the - Gold - en West and you, I'm com - ing back to Cal - i - for - nia to my lit - tle girl so true. How well I re - mem - ber the tear in your eye, the day that I

left you and kissed you good-bye I'm com-ing back to Cal-i-for-nia,

to the Gold-en West and you.

Honey girl don't sigh, dry those tears, don't cry, I'll be coming back some day;
Though you write, you're blue, little girl so true, because you know I'm far away.
You know I love you best, girl of the Golden West, and the Land of the Western Sun.
I'll pack up right away for the old U.S.A., for when the war is won,

CHORUS
I'm coming back to California, to the Golden West and you,
I'm coming back to California to my little girl so true.
How well I remember the tear in your eye, the day that I left you and kissed you goodbye.
I'm coming back to California, to the Golden West and you.

California's throng will step right along from Paris to Berlin,
Lads from Albuquerque will do some mighty work, declare the gang from Phoenix in,
The Denver bunch has "Pep," you know the Mormon's "Rep," the combination spells EX-CEL. (XL)
Our folks will all hear us shout, while we knock Huns about, when Wilhelm's in his cell,

CHORUS
We're coming back to California,
to the Golden West and you,
We're coming back to California,
where the Sunshine Division grew,
After wading through Europe and doing our bit,
the road to the West is the trail we will hit,
We're coming back to California,
to the Golden West and you.

"Sunshine Division" Camp Kearny, California "We're Coming Back to California"

Senza I Brazzi E Fuori

California has always had an abundant supply of cheap labor. First the Indians at the missions, then the Chinese on the railroads and the farms. After the Chinese were driven from the farms during the 1890s, they were replaced by a diverse group of immigrants from Japan, Portugal, Armenia, India and Italy. These immigrants brought songs from the old country.

This song came to California from Sicily. We learned it from Ralph Comito, who learned it from his mother,

Josephine Comito. The words mean: "Mother, summer is here and I want to be married. I would like a sleeveless dress, a pair of shoes and a pretty hat, for that is the style. Without a sleeveless dress I cannot get married. My boy friend is waiting for me and we want to make love tonight in this beautiful city. Even though my father is a shoemaker and not a lawyer, still I want to be in style even though the price is costly. I'm getting older and I must get married."

Canning Factory, Selma

Senza I Brazzi E Fuori

Words and Music: Anonymous.

Mamma la stati vima e mi la affari
N'a vesticeda cu li brazzie fora.
Un paru di scarpini ma accattare
Un cappedduzzu cha chista e la moda
Si su a to fighia vo maritari.

CHORUS
E senza brazzi fora nun mi pozu maritari,
U zitu ma speta ancora - a idu ma pighiari
Che bella sta cita, e la muri sava fa,
E senza brazzi fora, non mi pozu marita.

Benchi con sungnu fighia da vucatu
Sugnu n'a fighia du mastru scarparu,
E vera cha lu lussu custa caru
E papa e scarparu e lu putemo face
Sugnu granduzza e maiu a maritari. CHORUS

The Preacher and the Slave

Some labor organizing among California farm workers occurred in the early 1900s, especially by the Industrial Workers of the World. By 1913, California's IWW membership had grown to five thousand, and they created an influence far greater than their numbers. Singing was one of their best tools for agitation and organization. IWW members were called "wobblies," and wobbly songs were sung throughout the state. Their best songwriters were Ralph Chaplin and Joe Hill, and their most famous songs were Chaplin's "Solidarity Forever" and Hill's "The Preacher and the Slave."

The tune is from J. P. Webster's popular revival song "The Sweet Bye And Bye."

The Preacher and the Slave

Words: Joe Hill. Music: J. P. Webster.

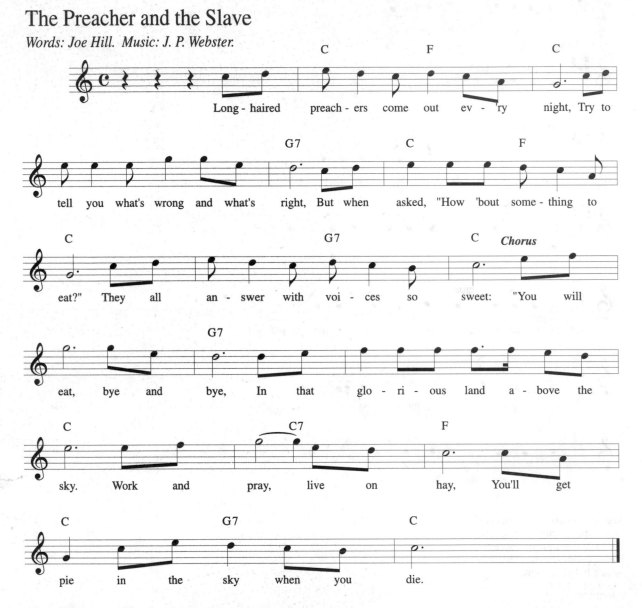

Long-haired preachers come out every night,
Try to tell you what's wrong and what's right,
But when asked, "How about something to eat?"
They all answer with voices so sweet:

CHORUS
You will eat, bye and bye,
In that glorious land above the sky.
Work and pray, live on hay,
You'll get pie in the sky when you die.

And the starvation army they play,
And they sing and they clap and they pray,
Till they get all your coin on the drum,
Then they'll tell you, when you're on the bum:
CHORUS

When you fight hard for children and wife,
Try to get something good in this life,
"You're a sinner, and a bad man," they'll tell,
"When you die you will sure go to hell." CHORUS

Working men of all countries unite,
Side by side we for freedom will fight,
When the world and its wealth we have gained,
To the grafters we'll sing this refrain:

LAST CHORUS
You will eat, bye and bye,
When you've learned how to cook and to fry,
Chop some wood, 'twill do you good,
And you'll eat in the sweet bye and bye.

The Mower's Song

Japanese farm workers who came to California between 1890 and 1910 presented a different challenge to California's farmers. They bought land and began to compete. They introduced new rice growing techniques, and were soon producing yields valued at three and a half times the yields on other California farms, on land that had been considered worthless. The California State Legislature responded to this by passing the Alien Land Law, to prevent the Japanese from owning land. However, by this time, many of the Japanese farmers had children born in the United States, so they obtained title to the farms in their children's names. As they worked in California's fields, they sang, "We have finished mowing on the mountain. Tomorrow we'll be in the fields cutting down the rice stalks."

Japanese Workers Gathering Cucumbers, San Joaquin Valley

The Mower's Song
Words and Music: Anonymous.

Koko no Yamano
Kari bosha su-un dayo
Asu wa Ta-am bo de
E E Ine karo ka yo

Canción Mixteca

The Mexican Revolution of 1910 to 1920 resulted in the migration of a quarter of a million Mexican refugees to California. They were welcomed on the farms because of the labor shortage brought on by World War I. By the 1920s, Mexican immigrants dominated California's farm labor force. Many of them sang songs of home.

The words mean:

How far away I am from the land of my birth. Intense nostalgia permeates my consciousness. Oh land of the sun, now so distant, I live without light, without love. I find myself so alone and sad, like a leaf in the wind. I want to cry, I want to die from deep emotion.

Canción Mixteca

Words and Music: Anonymous.

Qué lejos estoy del suelo donde he nacido,
Intensa nostalgia invade mi pensamiento,
Y al verme tan solo y triste cual hoja al viento,
Quisiera llorar, quisiera morir, de sentimiento.

¡O tierra del sol! suspiro por verte,
Ahora que lejos, yo vivo sin luz, sin amor.
Y al verme tan solo y triste cual hoja al viento,
Quisiera llorar, quisiera morir, de sentimiento.

Los Deportados

During the early 1930s, California's Mexican farm workers began organizing labor unions. When they went on strike in the Imperial Valley cantaloupe fields, the farm owners fought back. They brought 35,000 workers from the Philippines, and then deported thousands of Mexican workers, temporarily ending Mexican domination of California's farm labor force. As they left California, the Mexican workers sang "Los Deportados," a song from the early 1900s.

The words mean:

I'm going to tell you a story about all that I suffered when I left my country to come here. At 10:00 pm the train started to go. My mother said, "What a thankless train, to take my son away." When we arrived at Juárez, the officials said, "How much money do you have, to take into this country?" I said, "I have enough money to emigrate." They said, "Your money is worthless." Today they are creating a storm, and without consideration women, children and old people are being deported. Goodbye, my dear countrymen, now it's time to leave, but we are not bandits, we came here to work. There is hope now in my country, the revolution is over. Let's go my dear friends, we'll get a good reception in our beautiful country.

Loading Cantaloupe,
Imperial Valley

Los Deportados

Words and Music: Anonymous.

A - diós, pai - sa - nos quer - i - dos, A - diós, pai - san - os quer -
i - dos, Ya nos van a de - por - tar, Pe -
ro, no so - mos ban - di - dos, Pe - ro, no so - mos ban - di - dos, Ven -
i - mos a cam - e - llar.

Voy a contarles, señores,
Voy a contarles señores,
Todo lo que yo sufrí,
Cuando deje yo a mi Patria,
Cuando deje yo a mi Patria,
Por venir a ese país.

Serian las diez de la noche,
Serian las diez de la noche,
Comenzo un tren a silvar;
Oi que dijo mi madre
Hay viene ese tren ingrato
Que a mi hijo se va a llevar.

Llegamos por fin a Juárez,
Llegamos por fin a Juárez,
Ahi fue mi a apuración
Que donde va, que donde viene,
Cuanto dinero tiene
Para entrar a está nación.

Señores, traigo dinero,
Señores, traigo dinero,
Para poder emigrar,
Su dinero nada vale,
Su dinero nada vale,
Te tenemos que bañar.

Hoy traen la gran polvadera
Hoy traen la gran polvadera
Y sin consideración,
Mujeres, niños, y ancianos
Los llevan a la frontera
Los echan de esa nación.

Adiós, paisanos queridos,
Adiós, paisanos queridos,
Ya nos van a deportar,
Pero no somos bandidos,
Pero no somos bandidos,
Venimos a camellar.

Los espero allá en mi tierra,
Los espero allá en mi tierra,
Ya no hay mas revolución;
Vámanos cuates queridos
Seremos bien recibidos
En nuestra bella nación.

So Long, It's Been Good to Know You

Three generations of poor farming practices in the plains states, including the lack of terracing and contour plowing, the lack of windbreaks, and the lack of crop rotation, resulted in major ecological disasters in the 1930s. On Armistice Day, 1933, the first great dust storm hit South Dakota. Farmers described the storm as a wall of dirt, cold and blacker than night. The dirt penetrated eyes, ears, nose and lungs. Fields were covered with drifting sand. Roads were obliterated. Farm machinery and fences were buried. Only the roofs of sheds protruded above the sand.

Later that year, this description would apply to farms all the way from the Texas panhandle to the Canadian border. During the next two years, thousands of square miles were laid waste, and thousands of farmers abandoned their homes. Many of them migrated to California.

Woody Guthrie was inspired to write this song after experiencing a major dust storm in Pampa, Texas, on April 14, 1935.

So Long, It's Been Good to Know Yuh

Words and Music: Woody Guthrie.

TRO - © Copyright 1940 (Renewed) 1950 (Renewed) 1963 (Renewed) Folkways Music Publishers, Inc., New York, NY. Used by permission.

I've sung this song, but I'll sing it a-gain, Of the place that I lived on the wild, wind-y plains. In the month called A-pril, the coun-ty called Gray, And here's what all of the peo-ple there say: So long, it's been good to know ye, So long, it's been good to know ye, So long, it's been good to know ye, This dust-y old dust is a-get-ting my home, And I've got to be drift-ing a-long.

Dust Bowl Version:

I've sung this song, but I'll sing it again,
Of the place that I lived on the wild windy plains.
In the month called April, the county called Gray,
And here's what all of the people there say:

CHORUS
So long, it's been good to know ye,
So long, it's been good to know ye,
So long, it's been good to know ye,
This dusty old dust is a-getting my home,
And I've got to be drifting along.

A dust storm hit and it hit like thunder;
It dusted us over and it covered us under;
It blocked out the traffic and blocked out the sun.
Straight for home all the people did run. CHORUS

We talked of the end of the world, and then
We'd sing a song, and then sing it again;
We'd sit for an hour and not say a word,
And then these words would be heard: CHORUS

The sweethearts sat in the dark and they sparked,
They hugged and they kissed in that dusty old dark.
They sighed and they cried, hugged and kissed,
Instead of marriage they talked like this: Honey CHORUS

Now, the telephone rang and it jumped off the wall;
That was the preacher a-making his call.
He said, "Kind friend, this may be the end;
You've got your last chance of salvation of sin." CHORUS

The churches was jammed, and the churches was packed,
And that dusty old dust storm blowed so black;
The preacher could not read a word of his text,
And he folded his specs and he took up collection, said: CHORUS

Popular Version:

I've sung this song, but I'll sing it again,
Of the people I've met and the places I've been.
Of some of the troubles that bothered my mind,
And a lot of good people that I've left behind, saying:

CHORUS
So long, it's been good to know ye,
So long, it's been good to know ye,
So long, It's been good to know ye,
What a long time since I've been home,
And I've got to be drifting along.

The sweethearts sat in the dark and they sparked,
They hugged and kissed in that dusty old dark,
They sighed and cried, hugged and kissed,
Instead of marriage they talked like this: Honey CHORUS

I went to your fam'ly and asked them for you.
They all said, "Take her, oh, take her, please do!
She can't cook or sew and she won't scrub your floor,"
So I put on my hat and tiptoed out the door, saying: CHORUS

I walked down the street to the grocery store.
It was crowded with people both rich and both poor.
I asked the man how his butter was sold;
He said, "One pound of butter for two pounds of gold." I said: CHORUS

My telephone rang and it jumped off the wall.
That was the preacher a-making a call.
He said, "We're waitin' to tie the knot;
You're gettin' married, believe it or not!"

The church it was jammed, the church it was packed;
The pews were so crowded from front to the back.
A thousand friends waited to kiss my new bride,
But I was so anxious I rushed her outside. Told them: CHORUS

If You Ain't Got the Do Re Mi

From 1933 to 1937, migrants from the dust bowl states poured into California. They were called "Okies," short for Oklahomans. Citizens in urban areas became concerned about feeding and housing the dust bowl refugees. In response to this concern, the city of Los Angeles posted 125 policemen at ports of entry, many miles from Los Angeles, turning away people whom they considered unemployable or undesirable.

Do Re Mi

Words and Music: Woody Guthrie.

Lots of folks back east they say, leav-in' home, ev-'ry day,

Beat-in' the hot old dust-y way to the Cal-i-for-nia line.

'Cross the des-ert sands they roll, get-ting out of that old dust bowl, they

Think they're go-in' to a sug-ar bowl but here is what they find:

Now the po-lice at the port of en-try

say, "You're num-ber four-teen-thou-sand for to-

Chorus

day." Oh, if you ain't got the do-re-

mi, folks, if you ain't got the do-re-

mi, Why, you bet-ter go-back to beau-ti-ful

Tex-as, O-kla-ho-ma, Kan-sas, Geor-gia, Ten-nes-

see. Ca-li-for-nia is a gar-den of

E - den, a par-a-dise to live in or see, But be-lieve it or not you won't find it so hot, if you ain't got the do - re - mi.

Lots of folks back east they say, leavin' home every day,
Beatin' the hot old dusty way to the California line.
'Cross the desert sands they roll, getting out of that old dust bowl,
They think they're going to a sugar bowl but here is what they find:
Now the police at the port of entry say, "You're number fourteen thousand for today."

CHORUS
Oh, if you ain't got the do re mi, folks, if you ain't got the do re mi,
Why, you better go back to beautiful Texas, Oklahoma, Kansas, Georgia, Tennessee.
California is a garden of Eden, a paradise to live in or see,
But believe it or not you won't find it so hot, if you ain't got the do re mi.

If you want to buy a home or a farm, that can't do nobody harm,
Or take your vacation by the mountains or sea,
Don't swap your old cow for a car, you'd better stay right where you are;
You'd better take this little tip from me.
'Cause I look through the want ads every day, but the headlines in the papers always say: CHORUS

Many of the people who crossed the border into California sought work on farms. The huge corporate farms needed large numbers of workers for the short harvest season. It was a common practice to distribute thousands of handbills to fill a few hundred temporary jobs. These recruiting methods often attracted three or four times the number of pickers needed, and the farm corporations could hire people hungry and desperate enough to accept starvation wages. At the same time, fertile fields lay unproductive to keep profits up. Carloads of oranges were dumped on the ground. Hungry people traveled for miles to take the fruit, but were held back while kerosene was squirted on the oranges. Potatoes were dumped into the river, and guards posted to keep people from retrieving them. Pigs were slaughtered, dumped into ditches, and covered with quicklime.

The Great Depression took its toll. By 1932, twenty-five percent of California's citizens were on relief. In 1934, nearly a million voters supported gubernatorial candidate Upton Sinclair and his socialist End Poverty In California program, but Sinclair lost to conservative Frank Merriam. In 1938, Culbert L. Olson became governor, proposing New Deal reforms. He was unsuccessful in implementing them.

World War Two, Songs of the Cities

I LOVE YOU CALIFORNIA

Words by F. B. SILVERWOOD
Music by A. F. FRANKENSTEIN

DEDICATED
AL MALAIKAH
TEMPLE
LOS ANGELES

I Love You California

"I Love You California" was published in 1913. By Senate Concurrent Resolution 29, adopted by the legislature and filed with the Secretary of State on April 26, 1951, it became the official California state song.

I Love You California

Words: F. B. Silverwood. Music: A. F. Frankenstein.

fume, It is here na-ture gives of her rar - est. It is

Home Sweet Home to me, And I know when I die I shall

breathe my last sigh For my sun - ny Cal - i - for - nia.

I love you California, you're the greatest state of all,
I love you in the winter, summer, spring and in the fall,
I love your fertile valleys, your dear mountains I adore,
I love your grand old ocean and I love her rugged shore.

CHORUS
Where the snow crowned Golden Sierras keep their watch o'er the valleys bloom,
It is there I would be in our land by the sea, every breeze bearing rich perfume,
It is here nature gives of her rarest, it is Home Sweet Home to me,
And I know when I die I shall breathe my last sigh for my sunny California.

I love your redwood forests, love your fields of yellow grain,
I love your summer breezes and I love your winter rain,
I love you, land of flowers; land of honey, fruit and wine.
I love you, California; you have won this heart of mine. CHORUS

I love your old gray Missions, love your vineyards stretching far,
I love you, California, with your Golden Gate ajar,
I love your purple sunsets, love your skies of azure blue.
I love you, California; I just can't help loving you. CHORUS

I love you, Catalina, you are very dear to me,
I love you, Tamalpais, and I love Yosemite.
I love you, Land of Sunshine, half your beauties are untold.
I love you in my childhood, and I'll love you when I'm old. CHORUS

Rosie the Riveter

When America entered World War II, California's dust bowl refugees were absorbed into the armed services and into wartime production. Southern California dominated the aircraft industry, the San Francisco Bay Area dominated the ship building industry. California was also a major producer of oil, steel, rubber, machinery and electrical equipment.

With so many men entering the armed forces, women were recruited to perform jobs that had been traditionally held by men: riveters, drill press operators, machine tool operators and welders. Women worked in factories producing bombs, tanks, ships and airplanes. They discovered that they could earn wages high enough to make them independent, and the seeds were sown for the women's movements that followed.

Rusty's mother, Bea Donals Wilmsmeier, worked for Northrop Aircraft, Inc. as a fabricator, riveter and assembler during World War II. She was a very attractive young woman, and became a recruiter for Northrop, helping to convince other women to become aircraft workers.

Rosie the Riveter

Words and Music: Redd Evans and John Jacob Loeb.

All the day long wheth-er rain or shine, she's a part of the as-sem-bly line, She's mak-in' his-to-ry, work-in' for vic-to-ry, Ros-ie the riv-et-er Keeps a sharp look out for sab-o-tage, sit-tin' up there on the fu-se-lage, That lit-tle frail can do more than a male can do, Ro-sie the riv-et-er. Ros-ie's got a boy friend Char-lie, Char-lie he's a ma-rine, Ro-sie is pro-tec-ting Char-lie, Work-in' o-ver-time on the riv-e-ting ma-chine, When they gave her a pro-

duc-tion E, she was as proud as a girl could be, There's some-thing true a-bout,

red, white and blue a-bout Ro-sie the riv-e-ter.

All the day long whether rain or shine, she's a part of the assembly line,
She's makin' history, workin' for victory, Rosie the riveter.
Keeps a sharp lookout for sabotage, sittin' up there on the fuselage,
That little frail can do more than a male can do, Rosie the riveter.
Rosie's got a boyfriend Charlie, Charlie he's a marine,
Rosie is protecting Charlie, workin' overtime on the riveting machine,
When they gave her a production E, she was as proud as a girl could be,
There's something true about, red, white and blue about Rosie the riveter.

Everyone stops to admire the scene, Rosie at work on the B-nineteen,
She's never twittery, nervous or jittery, Rosie the riveter.
What if she's smeared full of oil and grease, doin' her bit for the old Lend Lease,
She keeps the gang around, they love to hang around Rosie the riveter.
Rosie buys a lot of war bonds, that girl really has sense,
Wishes she could purchase more bonds, puttin' all her cash into National Defense,
Senator Jones who is "in the know," shouted these words on the radio,
"Berlin will hear about, Moscow will cheer about Rosie the riveter."

Rusty McNeil's mother, left, demonstrating aircraft assembly to recruit women for Northrop Aircraft - World War II.

Don't Fence Me In

World War II disrupted the lives of thousands of Japanese-Americans. One hundred and ten thousand people, two-thirds of them American citizens, were taken from their homes and interned in concentration camps. By early 1945, at the California internment camp at Manzanar, internees would gather together in the evening, stand behind the high fence and, with all its irony, sing Cole Porter's newly popular song "Don't Fence Me In."

Porter wrote the song in 1944, for the film *Hollywood Canteen*.

Manzanar

Don't Fence Me In   *Words and Music: Cole Porter.*

Wild Cat Kel-ley, look-ing might-y pale, was stand-ing by the sher-iff's side, And when that sher-iff said, "I'm send-ing you to jail,"

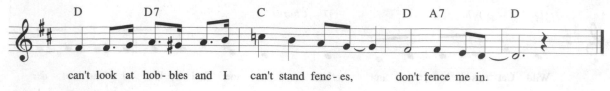

can't look at hob-bles and I can't stand fenc-es, don't fence me in.

Wild Cat Kelly, looking mighty pale, was standing by the sheriff's side,
And when that sheriff said "I'm sending you to jail," Wild Cat raised his head and cried:

CHORUS
Oh give me land lots of land under starry skies above, don't fence me in,
Let me ride through the wide open country that I love, don't fence me in.
Let me be by myself in the evening breeze, listen to the murmur of the cottonwood trees,
Send me off forever but I ask you please, don't fence me in.
Just turn me loose, let me straddle my old saddle underneath the western skies,
On my cayuse, let me wander over yonder till I see the mountains rise.
I want to ride to the ridge where the west commences, gaze at the moon until I lose my senses,
Can't look at hobbles and I can't stand fences, don't fence me in.

Wild Cat Kelly, back again in town, was sitting by his sweetheart's side,
And when his sweetheart said "Come on, let's settle down," Wild Cat raised his head and cried: CHORUS

442nd Infantry

Despite the internment, thousands of Japanese-Americans volunteered for military duty in the armed services. The armed forces were still segregated at that time, and most of the Japanese-American soldiers served in the 100th Infantry Battalion, and the 442nd Regimental Combat Team. The combat records of these two outfits were unsurpassed by any other group during the war. The slogan of the 442nd was "go for broke," a Hawaiian expression which meant "bet everything you have." Daniel Betsui, who was killed in action in Italy, wrote this song.

We learned this version from Frank Fukuzawa. He explained that each company in the 442nd inserted the name of its own company into the song. They sang the song to the tune of Irving Berlin's popular World War II song "This Is The Army Mr. Jones."

442nd Infantry
Words: Daniel Betsui. Music: Irving Berlin.

Four-forty-second Infantry
We're the boys from Fox Company,
We're fighting for you and the red, white and blue,
Up to the front and back to Honolululu.

Fighting for dear old Uncle Sam,
Go for broke, and we don't give a damn,
We've got the Hun at the point of a gun
And the victory will soon be won.

The official song of the 442nd was called "Go For Broke," written by private first class Harry Hamada in 1944, dedicated to Colonel Charles Pierce, first commanding officer of the 442nd.

"Let us go for broke" were the first words we spoke,
Umua lana kilu, forward to victory.
Let us fight, fight, fight, God will protect the right.
Nothing to fear, we're going to win this strife,
We are proud to wear the colors of our freedom,
Blood and tears won't be shed in vain,
Until peace is won there is so much to be done.
Shoot the works and let us go for broke.

El Soldado Razo

Thousands of Californians of Mexican descent also volunteered for military service. As they boarded the troop trains, they sang "El Soldado Razo."

The words mean:

I'm going as a soldier without rank, joining the file of young men who are leaving as their sweethearts cry at their departure. My only regret is leaving my mother alone. My Virgin of Guadalupe will protect my flag. When I find myself in battle far away from my land, I will prove that my race knows how to die anywhere. Tomorrow I will leave early to start a new day. Here goes another Mexican that is going to play with his life, saying, "Long live his country." Virgin Morena, take care of my mother until I return.

El Soldado Razo

Words and Music: Leal Felipe Valdez.

Me voy de sol - da - do ra - zo voy a in - gre - sar a las fi - las, Con los val - ien - tes mu - cha - chos que de - jan ma - dres quer - i - das que de - jan no - vias llo - ran - do, llo - ran - do su des - pe - di - da.

Chorus

Vir - gen ben - di - ta, mán - da - le tu con - sue - lo, Nun - ca ja - más per - mi - tas que me la ro - be el cie - lo.

Me voy de soldado razo voy a ingresar a las filas,
Con los valientes muchachos que dejan madres queridas
Que dejan novias llorando, llorando su despedida.

Voy a la guerra contento ya tengo rifle y pistola,
Ya volveré de sargento cuando se acabe la bola,
No más una cosa siento dejar a mi madre sola.

CHORUS
Virgen bendita mándale tu consuelo,
Nunca jamás permitas que me la robe el cielo.

Me virgen Guadalupana protegerá mi bandera,
Y cuando me halle en campaña muy lejos ya de me tierra
Les probaré que mi raza sabe morir donde quiera.

Mañana salgo temprano al despuntar nuevo día,
Voy a la guerra temprano esto dice un mexicano
Y se despide cantando que viva la Patria mía.

LAST CHORUS
Virgen morena, mi madre te encomiendo,
Cuídala, que es muy buena, cuídala mientras vuelvo.

Plane Wreck at Los Gatos

Wartime demands for workers and fighting men created an acute shortage of farm workers in California. During the harvest season in 1942, as a temporary stopgap, Ventura County secondary school students attended school on Mondays, Wednesdays and Fridays, and picked crops on Tuesdays, Thursdays and Saturdays. That same year, the United States government and the Mexican government worked out a plan whereby the Department of Agriculture would import, feed and house farm workers from Mexico on a temporary basis, creating what came to be known as the "bracero" program. Bracero means "strong arm" in Spanish. California's growers liked the system, and it continued in force after the war ended. Along with the legal braceros came a steady stream of illegal immigrants from Mexico, also eager to work in California's fields.

Many Californians harbored a deep prejudice against Mexicans and Californians of Mexican descent, despite their contributions on the battlefields and on the farms. In 1948, a planeload of farm workers being deported to Mexico crashed near Los Gatos, California, killing everyone on board. The radio announcement stated that it was no great tragedy because they were "just deportees." American folk poet Woody Guthrie, incensed over the callousness of the statement, wrote the song "Plane Wreck At Los Gatos."

The song is also known by the names "Deportee" and "Goodbye Juan."

Plane Wreck at Los Gatos (Deportee)

Words: Woody Guthrie. Music: Martin Hoffman.

TRO - © Copyright 1961 (Renewed) 1963 (Renewed) Ludlow Music, Inc., New York, NY. Used by permission.

The crops are all in and the peach - es are rot - t'ning.
The or - an - ges piled in their cre - o - sote dumps.
You're fly - ing 'em back to the Mex - i - can bor - der, To
pay all their mon - ey to wade back a - gain. Good -
bye to my Juan, good - bye Ro - sa - li - ta, a - diós mis a -
mi - gos, Je - sús y Ma - rí - a; You won't have your

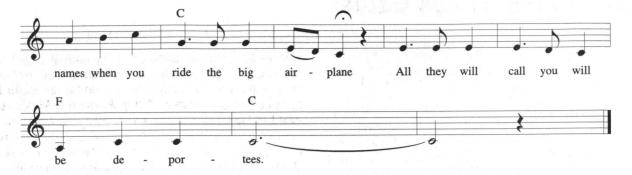

names when you ride the big air - plane All they will call you will

be de - por - tees.

The crops are all in, the peaches are rott'ning.
The oranges piled in their creosote dumps.
You're flying 'em back to the Mexican border,
To pay all their money to wade back again.

CHORUS
Goodbye to my Juan, goodbye, Rosalita,
Adiós mis amigos, Jesús y María,
You won't have your names when you ride the big airplane,
All they will call you will be, deportees.

My father's own father, he waded that river,
They took all the money he made in his life;
My brothers and sisters came working the fruit trees,
And they rode the truck till they took down and died. CHORUS

Some of us are illegal, and some are not wanted,
Our work contract's out and we have to move on;
Six hundred miles to that Mexican border,
They chase us like outlaws, like rustlers, like thieves. CHORUS

We died in your hills, we died in your deserts,
We died in your valleys and died on your plains,
We died 'neath your trees and we died in your bushes.
Both sides of the river, we died just the same. CHORUS

The sky plane caught fire over Los Gatos canyon,
A fireball of lightning, and shook all our hills,
Who are all these friends, all scattered like dry leaves?
The radio says they are just deportees. CHORUS

Is this the best way we can grow our big orchards?
Is this the best way we can grow our good fruit?
To fall like dry leaves to rot on my topsoil
And be called by no name except deportees? CHORUS

Kumbaya

Public pressure forced the termination of the bracero program in 1964. For the first time in California's history there was no readily available supply of cheap farm labor. In 1965 the Agricultural Workers Organizing Committee (AWOC), composed mostly of Filipino-Americans, began a strike against thirty-three grape growers in the Delano area of the San Joaquin Valley. Cesar Chavez's National Farm Workers Association, composed mostly of Mexican Americans, joined forces with AWOC. The strike resulted in the unionization of a number of major farms in California. A new body of song emerged, with new words sung to familiar American and Mexican melodies, in English and Spanish.

Picking Cantaloupe, Brawley

Kumbaya

Words and Music: Anonymous.

We are toiling, Lord, in the field,
We are toiling, Lord, in the field,
We are toiling, Lord, in the field,
Oh Lord, kumbaya, oh Lord, kumbaya.

CHORUS
Kumbaya my Lord, kumbaya,
Kumbaya my Lord, kumbaya,
Kumbaya my Lord, kumbaya,
Oh Lord, kumbaya, oh Lord, kumbaya.

Make them listen, Lord, kumbaya,
Make them listen, Lord, kumbaya,
Make them listen, Lord, kumbaya,
Oh Lord, kumbaya, oh Lord, kumbaya. CHORUS

Time is going Lord, kumbaya,
Time is going Lord, kumbaya,
Time is going Lord, kumbaya,
Oh Lord, kumbaya, oh Lord, kumbaya. CHORUS

Nosotros Venceremos

"Nosotros Venceremos" is "We Shall Overcome" sung in Spanish, from the Civil Rights movement of the 1960s. United Farm Workers members sang this song in the fields, at union meetings and on their 250 mile march from Delano to Sacramento in 1966.

The words mean:

We shall overcome, we shall overcome, we shall overcome some day. Oh, deep in my heart I do believe we shall overcome some day.

Nosotros Venceremos

Words and Music: Anonymous.

| C | F | C | Am | C | F |

No - so - tros ven - ce - re - mos, No - so - tros ven - ce -

| C | Am | C | F | Am | G7 |

re - mos, No - so - tros ven - ce - re - mos,

| C | F | C | Am | F | C |

Oh en mi cor - a - zón, Yo cre -

| Am | C | F | C | G7 | C | F | C |

o No - so - tros ven - ce - re - mos.

Nosotros venceremos,
Nosotros venceremos,
Nosotros venceremos,
O en mi corazón
Yo creo
Nosotros venceremos.

Farm Workers' 250 mile march to Sacramento, 1966

Santa Maria (My Old Home Town)

California songs reflect great pride in the state's cities and towns.

The composer, Frank Hayes, played the theater organ for silent movies in Santa Maria's Gaiety Theater during the 1920s. He was also bandmaster and director of the Santa Maria Elks Boys Band, and dedicated his song to Troop Three of the Boy Scouts. The song was published in 1923.

Santa Maria (My Old Home Town)

Words and Music: Frank P. Hayes.

I've trav-eled quite a lot in ev-'ry nook and spot, I've been in most ev-'ry for-eign land, I've been East and West, North and South and all the rest, I've seen cit-ies that were great and grand, But there's a lit-tle spot I long to see, A place that's al-ways Home sweet Home to me, be-lieve me

Chorus San-ta Ma-ri-a is my old "Home" town, And when I get back there I'll stay, There are no sky-scrap-ers on its main

street, The sun shines there most ev-'ry day,

A heart-y wel-come al-ways waits you there, A smile will greet you nev-er a frown,

I'll build a-lit-tle nest in a lit-tle place out West, In San-ta Ma-ri-a, my old home town.

SANTA MARIA
(My Old Home Town)

WORDS
&
MUSIC
BY

Frank P. Hayes

Organist of
GAIETY
Theatre

Published by
J. Hilliard Wright, O. D.
Santa Maria, California

Frank P.Hayes

I've traveled quite a lot in every nook and spot,
I've been in most every foreign land,
I've been East and West, North and South and all the rest,
I've seen cities that were great and grand,
But there's a little spot I long to see,
A place that's always Home Sweet Home to me, believe me

CHORUS
Santa Maria is my old "Home" town,
And when I get back there I'll stay,
There are no sky scrapers on its main street,
The sun shines there most every day.
A hearty welcome always waits you there,
A smile will greet you never a frown,
I'll build a little nest in a little place out West,
In Santa Maria, my old home town.

I've been to gay Paree and sunny Italy,
England, Ireland, Spain and Mexico,
Been in China too, seen the King of Timbuctoo,
In Russia where the Bolshevikis grow,
I've even seen the tomb of old King Tut,
Believe me I would rather own a Hut Out West in CHORUS

Brawley, the World's Largest City Beneath the Level of the Sea

The city of Brawley in the Imperial Valley, is located 113 feet below sea level. Here is Brawley's song, written to celebrate the city's First Annual Fiesta, held November 29, 1940.

Brawley, the World's Largest City Beneath the Level of the Sea

Words: R.M.Z. Amen. Music: R.M.Z. Amen and Collaborators.

In that mag - ic car - pet coun - try past the blue of Sal - ton Sea, Lies a charm - ing home sweet home - land where I ev - er long to be, Pan - o - ra - mic is its beau - ty na - ture spreads her ver - y best, And en - chant - ing - ly sur - rounds us here in Braw - ley Heav - en blest.

Chorus Braw - ley, The World's Larg - est Ci - ty be - neath the lev - el of the sea! - - - Braw - ley the World's Larg - est Ci - ty in point of in - 'trest to me! With your palm trees and your flow - ers, Gold - en wealth of sun - ny hours, o Braw - ley the World's Larg - est Ci - ty, you are top of the world to me.

In that magic carpet country past the blue of Salton Sea,
Lies a charming home sweet homeland where I ever long to be;
Panoramic is its beauty, nature spreads her very best,
And enchantingly surrounds us here in Brawley Heaven blest.

CHORUS
Brawley, the World's Largest City beneath the level of the sea!
Brawley, the World's Largest City in point of interest to me!
With your palm trees and your flowers, golden wealth of sunny hours,
O Brawley, the World's Largest City, you are top of the World to me.

Guarded well by desert, mountain, founded on a virgin soil,
Watered from a distant river tended by man's dreams and toil,
Doubly blest by golden sunshine and the glorious desert air,
It has blossomed into beauty of an "All Year Garden" fair. CHORUS

Simi Valley

Folk and country singer Jim St. Ours
wrote "Simi Valley" in 1978.

Simi Valley

Words and Music: Jim St. Ours.

Comin' over the waters across the divide, In
search of a homeland in which to reside, They settled in
mountains, they settled on plains, They settled in deserts
where it scarcely rains, And some of the people like you and like
me, Found a heavenly homeland called Simi Valley.

Chorus
From the rugged mountain walls to the green valley floor, With
wildflowers bloomin' each spring bringin' more From Rocky Peak
Pass to the cross on the hill, it's a valley we

love,   and   we al - ways   will.

Comin' over the waters across the divide,
In search of a homeland in which to reside;
They settled in mountains, they settled on plains,
They settled in deserts where it scarcely rains,
And some of the people, like you and like me,
Found a heavenly homeland called Simi Valley.

CHORUS
From the rugged mountain walls to the green valley floor,
With wild flowers bloomin' each spring bringin' more,
From Rocky Peak Pass to the cross on the hill,
It's a valley we love, and we always will.

The caves in the hills tell a story of old,
Of people who lived here a long time ago;
But now we see change in the face of the land,
By the passage of time and the progress of man,
We'll keep it unblemished the best that we can,
And let nature prevail in the service of man. CHORUS

L. A. River

In addition to extolling the virtues of the cities, Californians have no qualms about poking fun at some of the more bizarre features of their home towns.

We learned this song in the 1960s from folk/blues/gospel/pop singer Clabe Hangan.

Los Angeles River

L. A. River

Words and Music: Anonymous.

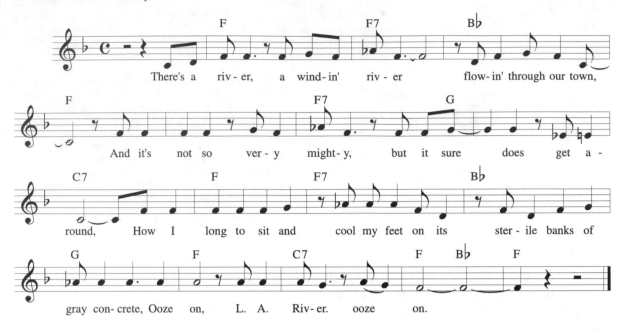

There's a river, a windin' river, flowin' through our town.
And it's not so very mighty, but it sure does get around,
How I long to sit and cool my feet on its sterile banks of gray concrete,
Ooze on, L.A. River, ooze on.

Well it's not so very mighty, and it's not so deep and wide,
But its current has a longing to stay at low, low tide,
And I thank the Lord that it's not blood red, but a peaceful, cool, green
algae instead,
Ooze on, L.A. River, ooze on.

Now when the thunder sounds like fury and the rain begins to fall,
I dream that the mighty crashing is that river's fearless roar,
But the sound I hear is not a dream, it's a motorcycle goin' upstream,
Ooze on, L.A. River, ooze on.

Well it hasn't any whitecaps, and it hasn't any fish,
To see it splash and ripple, it would be my fondest wish,
But it floats its load of sad debris from the mighty sewer to the mighty sea,
Ooze on, L.A. River, ooze on.
Ooze on, L.A. River, ooze on.

San Francisco
(Be Sure to Wear Some Flowers in your Hair)

A major generation gap emerged in the 1960s. Many of America's young people began questioning the values of their elders. They developed a counter-culture, centered in California, around the issues of the Vietnam War, free speech and civil rights. Many of the first members of the hippy movement lived in the Haight-Ashbury district in San Francisco. The uniform of the counter-culture was long hair, beads and sandals.

Many of the emerging rock 'n' roll groups were based in California. Scott McKenzie's recording of "San Francisco" was released in 1967. The song celebrates the "flower children" at the "love-in" at Haight-Ashbury.

San Francisco (Be Sure to Wear Some Flowers in your Hair)

Words and Music: John Phillips.

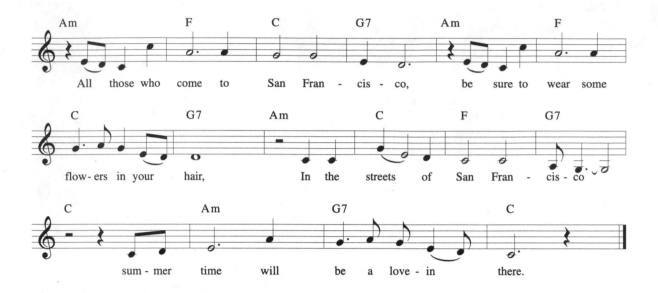

All those who come to San Fran - cis - co, be sure to wear some
flow- ers in your hair, In the streets of San Fran - cis - co
sum - mer time will be a love - in there.

If you're going to San Francisco, be sure to wear some flowers in your hair,
If you're going to San Francisco, you're going to meet some gentle people there.
All those who come to San Francisco, summertime will be a love-in there,
In the streets of San Francisco, gentle people with flowers in their hair.
All across the nation, such a strange vibration,
People in motion, people in motion,
There's a whole generation, with a new explanation,
People in motion, people in motion,
All those who come to San Francisco, be sure to wear some flowers in your hair,
In the streets of San Francisco, summertime will be a love-in there.

In 1962, California became the most populous state in the Union.
Despite the youth rebellion of the 1960s and '70s, the Watts riots of
1965, earthquakes, floods, mud slides, firestorms, smog, recessions
and crowded freeways, California's population tripled between 1950
and 1990. And, of course, twenty-first century California continues on
its often bumpy, constantly changing, but always optimistic journey.

Sources for and about songs sung in California:

Botkin, B. A. *A Treasury of Western Folklore*. New York: Crown Publishers, Inc., 1951.

Buttree, Julia M. *Rhythm of the Redman*. 67 West 44th Street, New York: A.S.Barnes & Company, 1930.

Cheney, Thomas E. *Mormon Songs From the Rocky Mountains*. Salt Lake City: University of Utah Press, 1981.

Cohen, Norm. *Long Steel Rail*. Urbana, Chicago, London: University of Illinois Press, 1981.

Dwyer, Richard A., Richard E. Lingenfelter and David Cohen. *The Songs of the Gold Rush*. Berkeley and Los Angeles: University of California Press, 1965.

Doerflinger, William Main. *Songs of the Sailor and Lumberman*. New York: The Macmillan Company, 1972.

Fife, Austin E. and Alta S. Fife. *Cowboy and Western Songs*. New York: Bramhall House, 1982.

Fillmore, Charles M. and J. H. Fillmore. *Songs of Might To Cheer the Fight Against the Blight Of Liquordom*. Cincinnati: Fillmore Music House, 1912.

Fletcher, Curly W. *Songs of the Sage*. Los Angeles: Frontier Publishing Company, 1931.

Greenway, John. *American Folksongs of Protest*. New York: A. S. Barnes & Company, Inc., 1953.

Guthrie, Woody. *The Nearly Complete Collection of Woody Guthrie Folksongs*. New York: Ludlow Music, Inc., 1963.

Pietroforte, Alfred. *Songs of the Yokuts and Paiutes*. Healdsburg, California: Naturegraph Press, 1965.

Levy, Lester S. *Flashes of Merriment - A Century of Humorous Songs in America 1805-1905*. Norman: University of Oklahoma Press, 1971.

Lingenfelter, Richard E., Richard A. Dwyer and David Cohen. *Songs of the American West*. Berkeley and Los Angeles: University of California Press, 1968.

Lomax, Alan, Woody Guthrie and Pete Seeger. *Hard Hitting Songs for Hard Hit People*. New York: Oak Publications, 1967.

Lomax, John A. and Alan Lomax. *American Ballads and Folk Songs*. New York: The Macmillan Company, 1934.

Sandburg, Carl. *The American Songbag*. New York: Harcourt, Brace, & Company, 1927.

Shull, Paul. *Music in the West*. Manhattan, Kansas: Sunflower University Press, 1983.

Stone, John A. *Put's Original California Songster*. 1855.

Picture Credits:

Page 1 Conquistador. By Frederick Remington. *Century Magazine*. New York. January, 1889.

Page 3 Quniáika - Mohave. Photo from Edward Sheriff Curtis: *Visions of a Vanishing Race* by Florence Curtis Graybill and Victor Boesen. Copyright © 1976 by Florence Curtis Graybill and Victor Boesen. Reprinted with permission of Multimedia Product Development, Inc., Chicago, Illinois. New large-format paperback edition available from the University of New Mexico Press, at (800) 249-7737.

Page 9 California Mode of Catching Cattle. Engraving in Alexander Forbes, *California: A History of Upper and Lower California*. London, 1839. Printed in *Land of Golden Dreams, California in the Gold Rush Decade, 1848-1858* by Peter Blodgett published by the Huntington Library (San Marino, 1999).

Page 15 A Family on the Overland Trail. Engraving by Frenzeny and Tavernier, *Harper's Weekly*, April 4, 1874. Printed in *The American West in the Nineteenth Century* by John Grafton published by Dover Publications, Inc. 1992.

Page 17 *Put's Original California Songster*. Published by D. E. Appleton & Co. San Francisco. 1855.

Page 20 Chagres River. Lithograph in Frank Marryat, *Mountains and Molehills, or, Recollections of a Burnt Journal*, London, 1855. Printed in *Land of Golden Dreams, California in the Gold Rush Decade, 1848-1858* by Peter Blodgett published by the Huntington Library (San Marino, 1999).

Page 21 Avalanche in the Sierra Nevada. Engraving by Lagarde Measom, *Frank Leslie's Illustrated Newspaper*, March 29, 1884. Printed in *The American West in the Nineteenth Century* by John Grafton published by Dover Publications, Inc. 1992.

Page 22 Crossing the Plains. Engraving by A. R.Waud, *Harper's Weekly*, December 23, 1871. Printed in *The American West in the Nineteenth Century* by John Grafton published by Dover Publications, Inc. 1992.

Page 24 California Prospector. *Illustrated News*, February 5, 1853. Printed in *The American West in the Nineteenth Century* by John Grafton published by Dover Publications, Inc. 1992.

Page 26 No Ladies at the Dance. Engraving by J. D. Borthwick, *Harper's Weekly*, October 3, 1857. Printed in *The American West in the Nineteenth Century* by John Grafton published by Dover Publications, Inc. 1992.

Page 30 Lunchtime at the Long Tom. Courtesy of the California History Room, California State Library, Sacramento, California.

Page 31 Chinese in San Francisco. Keystone-Mast Collection, UCR/California Museum of Photography, University of California at Riverside.

Page 33 James P. Beckwourth. Courtesy Denver Public Library, Western History Collection. Call # F9095.

Page 35 Proceedings of the Second Annual Convention of the Colored Citizens of the State of California, San Francisco, 1856. Printed in *Land of Golden Dreams, California in the Gold Rush Decade, 1848-1858* by Peter Blodgett published by the Huntington Library (San Marino, 1999).

Page 39 Ship *Glenesslin* ashore at Tillamook Head, Oregon. Courtesy San Francisco Maritime NHP Photographic Collection. Photo Number E3.6942n

Page 41 Mosa - Mohave. Photo from Edward Sheriff Curtis: *Visions of a Vanishing Race* by Florence Curtis Graybill and Victor Boesen. Copyright © 1976 by Florence Curtis Graybill and Victor Boesen. Reprinted with permission of Multimedia Product Development, Inc., Chicago, Illinois. New large-format paperback edition available from the University of New Mexico Press, at (800) 249-7737.

Page 43 Train in the Sierra Nevada Mountains. *Frank Leslie's Illustrated Newspaper*, April 27, 1878. Printed in *The American West in the Nineteenth Century* by John Grafton published by Dover Publications, Inc. 1992.

Page 44 Building the Central Pacific Engraving by A. R. Waud, *Harper's Weekly*, May 29, 1869. Printed in *The American West in the Nineteenth Century* by John Grafton published by Dover Publications, Inc. 1992.

Page 48 *The Struggle of the Mussel Slough Settlers.* California Historical Society, North Baker Research Library. Published by Visalia: Delta Printing Establishment, 1880.

Page 53 California Orange Grove. Keystone-Mast Collection, UCR/California Museum of Photography, University of California at Riverside.

Page 56 Herd of Sheep. Keystone-Mast Collection, UCR/California Museum of Photography, University of California at Riverside.

Page 58 Roping and Branding Calves. Engraving by W. A. Rogers, *Harper's Weekly*, October 6, 1883. Printed in *The American West in the Nineteenth Century* by John Grafton published by Dover Publications, Inc. 1992.

Page 63 Breaking Horses. Engravings by Jerome H. Smith and Charles M. Russell, *Frank Leslie's Illustrated Newspaper*, May 18, 1889. Printed in *The American West in the Nineteenth Century* by John Grafton published by Dover Publications, Inc. 1992.

Page 65 Republic Studios, Hollywood. Keystone-Mast Collection, UCR/California Museum of Photography, University of California at Riverside.

Page 67 *Songs of Might to Cheer the Fight Against the Blight Of Liquordom.* Published by Fillmore Music House, Cincinnati, Ohio. 1912.

Page 73 *He'd Have to Get Under - Get Out and Get Under.* Published by Maurice Abrahams Music Co. 1913.

Page 74 Touring Car. Keystone-Mast Collection, UCR/California Museum of Photography, University of California at Riverside.

Page 75 Early Automobile. Keystone-Mast Collection, UCR/California Museum of Photography, University of California at Riverside.

Page 77 Silent Movie Camera. Courtesy The Motion Picture Academy of Arts and Sciences, Center for Motion Picture Study, Margaret Herrick Library.

Page 81 Daniel Boone Silent Movie. Keystone-Mast Collection, UCR/California Museum of Photography, University of California at Riverside.

Page 85 Musicians in San Diego, 1916. Keystone-Mast Collection, UCR/California Museum of Photography, University of California at Riverside.

Page 87 *We're Coming Back to California.* Published by Sherman, Clay & Co. 1918.

Page 88 Canning Factory, Selma. Keystone-Mast Collection, UCR/California Museum of Photography, University of California at Riverside.

Page 91 Japanese Workers Gathering Cucumbers, San Joaquin Valley. Keystone-Mast Collection, UCR/California Museum of Photography, University of California at Riverside.

Page 93 Loading Cantaloupe, Imperial Valley. Keystone-Mast Collection, UCR/California Museum of Photography, University of California at Riverside.

Page 99 *I Love You, California.* Published by B. F. Silverwood. 1913.

Page 102 World War II Northrop Aircraft Recruiting Station. McNeil archives.

Page 104 Manzanar. Courtesy of the Bancroft Library, University of California, Berkeley.

Page 110 Picking Cantaloupe, Brawley. Keystone-Mast Collection, UCR/California Museum of Photography, University of California at Riverside.

Page 112 March to Sacramento. Printed in *Sing Out! The Folk Song Magazine.* Volume 16, Number 5, November, 1966.

Page 114 *Santa Maria (My Old Home Town).* Published by J. Hilliard Wright, O.D. 1923.

Page 117 Los Angeles River. Photo by Keith McNeil.

Index of songs:

Acknowledgements:

Our thanks to Darrin Schuck for assistance on musical notation, to Sonia Camacho, Joe Rael and David Cahueque for help in Spanish translations, to Dr. Sandra Kamusikiri for research on African-Americans in California, to John and Jenny Ysursa for Andre Madalen and the Basque translation, to Ralph Comito for Senza I Brazzi E Fuori and Sicilian translation, to Warren Sherk at the Motion Picture of Arts and Sciences, Center for Motion Picture Study, Margaret Herrick Library for silent movie music, to Mary, Sarah and Connie McNeil and Tom Johnson for proofreading and suggestions, to John Garrett Short for design work and layout, and to Sam Hinton, Clabe Hangan, Dick Holdstock, Allan MacLeod, Ted and Katie Moews, and all other friends and family members who have shared their music and knowledge with us over the years.

For pictures, our thanks go to Peter Blodgett and Peggy Park Bernal at the Huntington Library, Steven Thomas at the UCR/California Museum of Photography, Jennifer Thom and Laurie Swingle at the Denver Public Library, Scott Mendel at Multimedia Product Development, Ellen Harding at the California State Library, Susan Snyder at the Bancroft Library, Crissa Van Vleck at the California Historical Society and Bill Kooiman at the San Francisco Maritime National Historical Park.

For assistance in obtaining song permissions, we thank Dave Olsen at Warner Bros. Publications, Loretta Fellin at The Richmond Organization, Aida García-Cole at Music Sales Corporation and Fred Ahlert at Fred Ahlert Music Corporation.